WHAT I
LEARNED
ALONG
THE WAY

Thanks to Brian Levine and Elicia Pappalardo at Blinc International for their support and enthusiasm for this project, and to the staff of the Noosa Blue Resort. Thanks also to the team at New Holland Publishers for their hard work in getting this book to press, especially Fiona Schultz, who commissioned the project; writer Alan Whiticker; editor Kate Sherington, for wonderfully judged work; and Kim Pearce, for her beautiful design.

First published in 2013 by
New Holland Publishers
London • Sydney • Cape Town • Auckland
www.newhollandpublishers.com

The Chandlery, Unit 114, 50 Westminster Bridge Road, London, SE1 7QY
1/66 Gibbes Street Chatswood NSW 2067 Australia
Wembley Square First Floor Solan Road Gardens Cape Town 8001 South Africa
218 Lake Road Northcote Auckland New Zealand

A catalogue record of this book is available at the British Library and at the National Library of Australia.

ISBN: 9781742574776

10 9 8 7 6 5 4 3 2 1

Publisher: Fiona Schultz
Writer: Alan Whiticker
Project editor: Kate Sherington
Designer: Kimberley Pearce
Production director: Olga Dementiev
Printer: Toppan Leefung Printing Ltd (China)
Cover photo by Sheree McArthur Photography www.shereemcarthurphotography.com.au

Follow New Holland Publishers on
Facebook: www.facebook.com/NewHollandPublishers

WHAT I
LEARNED
ALONG
THE WAY

Dawn Fraser

contents

introduction

It's hard to believe Dawn Fraser has been part of the Australian story for almost six decades now, ever since she burst onto the national scene as a teenager at the 1956 Melbourne Olympics, winning gold medals in the 100m and the 4 x 100m freestyle relay. The self-described larrikin from the working class Sydney suburb of Balmain was thrust into the spotlight at the age of 19 and handled herself with confidence and aplomb.

After the Commonwealth Games in Cardiff in 1958, Dawn set her sights on representing Australia at a second Olympics. This in itself was a huge challenge in an era when young women were expected to marry and start a family. Instead, Dawn worked a number of jobs to support herself while she trained in her amateur sport. In Rome in 1960, she won gold in her pet event, the 100m freesytle, but was banned for 12 months by the Australian Swimming Union (ASU) for her 'refusal' to swim the butterfly leg of the medley relay. Dawn was determined to swim on. In 1962, she broke the magical minute mark for the 100m before starring at the Perth Commonwealth Games.

Then came the Tokyo Games. In 1964, Dawn became the first swimmer to win gold in the same event at three consecutive Olympics, but controversy was never far away. Two minor infringements – marching in the opening ceremony, and wearing an unofficial swimsuit in some races – saw her banned from competition for 10 years. Her decision to take part in an early morning prank to souvenir an Olympic flag at the Imperial Palace also cost her dearly. Dawn successfully sued the ASU and overturned the ban, but she lost the chance of a fourth straight gold at the 1968 Mexico Olympics.

Dawn has handled more than her fair share of tragedy. Her brother Donnie died at the age of 21 from leukemia; her beloved father passed away at the height of her career in 1961; and, as she prepared for an historic third Olympics in 1964, her mother was killed in a car accident in which Dawn was the driver. A failed marriage, post-career depression, an unsuccessful business and the day-to-day battles of single parenthood compounded the harshness of the bans handed down by swimming officialdom in her career. Yet she survived it all to claim her rightful place as a national sporting icon.

Each chapter of this book is supported by episodes from Dawn's amazingly full life. Offering gentle and considered advice for the next generation, Dawn opens up about the importance of family and friends, her career as a politician, and her long-lasting swimming legacy.

Here is someone who has truly learned a lot along the way.

chapter 1
Seek out challenges

IF YOU WERE A FAKE PERSON, IT WOULD BE VERY EASY TO FALL FLAT ON YOUR BACKSIDE AND LOSE A LOT OF FACE ON A REALITY TV SHOW LIKE *CELEBRITY APPRENTICE*. But I had nothing to lose.

I went on the show for two reasons – to earn some money, because I wanted to take my grandson Jackson on an overseas holiday, and to raise money for Riding for the Disabled on the Sunshine Coast, a charity that allows children with disabilities to work with horses. They were having trouble securing a place to work their magic – two farms they wanted to use had fallen through – and needed a lot of volunteers to make the activity work. We read about it in the local newspaper, and when my daughter Dawn-Lorraine suggested I do something to help, I decided to contact them. When I met the people running

Riding for the Disabled and saw all these great kids interacting with horses, I thought, *Wow, how good is this?* Being a horse lover and having a special bond with kids, I thought it was a great cause. The kids loved the interaction and the animals loved it as well. Horses are so intelligent; you could see them nudging the kids along and really caring for them.

I made my mind up then and there to challenge myself and try to raise some money for the charity. And then the offer to do *Celebrity Apprentice* came along. I decided to do it – maybe I would only last a week on the program, but that would be OK as long as I raised some money. I didn't know much about the program either. I'm a *CSI* and *Mentalist* fan, so prefer watching crime shows over reality TV. Put it this way, I won't be going on *Big Brother* any time soon! I knew once we started, though, that the competitor in me would quickly come out. I just hoped to be the project manager at some stage and show everyone what I could do.

I enjoyed meeting the other contestants in Sydney. I knew several of them already, and most of the others by reputation, but there were a couple of new faces there as well. Altogether, there were my fellow Olympians Stephanie Rice and John Stephenson, PR gurus Prue MacSween and Roxy Jacenko, TV types Dermott Brereton and Peter Everett, singers Brian Mannix, Rob Mills and Prinnie Stevens, boxer Jeff Fenech, reality star Layla Subritzky, comedian Peter Berner and dancer Kym Johnson. That cast was a real eye-opener and after only a couple of days I wondered what I'd got myself into. I was the oldest competitor by about 30 years, except for Prue MacSween, but I was determined to show what older Australians could achieve. I wanted to show people of any age, sitting at home on the lounge, who often can't find the time or motivation to get up and go for a walk, that if I could do it, so could they. I think I'm pretty fit and active for my age, and I want to keep it that way. It helps that I have a grandson who likes to play football and shoot hoops with me, and whom I take swimming and riding on his bike. Perhaps the different generations watching the show, I thought, would gain a new appreciation and respect for older Australians.

Well, as far as some of the contestants on the show went, that was easier said than done!

At the end of the first day, I went back to the hotel and gave myself a stern talking to. 'Dawn, you're doing this for charity! Don't let any of the other nonsense – the celebrity stuff, the difficult personalities – get in the way. Don't get involved in it.' Remembering that helped me to become a competitor again and focus on the challenges at hand. I thought I could do something positive on the show, by saying what was on my mind and being honest with everyone, and in the end, I stayed on *Celebrity Apprentice* much longer than I'd anticipated – I thought I'd be fired for sure.

For the most part, I think I got on well with the other people involved. Layla was lovely to work with; she came out of herself more as the show went along. Kym was a soft and gentle person. I loved Peter, a very sweet guy, and Brian was a lot of fun. He called me Joan throughout the show, because I reminded him of his mother-in-law. Jeff was Jeff – he pulled the odd sneaky trick and all Dermott wanted to do was show me photos of his girlfriend. Some of the others? Let's just say I won't be expecting a Christmas card from them!

I worked very hard on Father Chris Riley's 'Youth off the Streets' challenge. We had 24 hours to make over the Don Bosco Youth Centre that the charity uses, and I started on the backyard. I love gardening, so I knew exactly what I wanted to do and had everything planned, but then Max Markson, one of the advisers from the previous series, came in and ripped up the entire backyard. When I came back from shopping, it was like a quagmire, and I did my block. I had it ready to be mowed and fitted out with new plants, and I had to ask Roxy to lend me her work team to fix it, otherwise we wouldn't have been ready. It turned out very nicely, but it broke my heart when I first saw the mess that was made.

I was fired at the end of that challenge … well, sort of. My grandson Jackson and I were due to travel overseas on the night of the final, for the annual Laureus World Sports Awards in Rio de Janeiro. I had put our passports in to be processed weeks before, but the schedule was so hectic, I could not get a couple of hours to go and pick them up, as we were on call all day. On the Wednesday of the last week of the show, I finally asked the producer if I could go and get them. When she said there wasn't time, I wanted out. They told me I couldn't quit, so I asked her to tell CEO Mark Bouris to fire me that night.

That's why, when Mr Bouris asked, 'Dawn, who should I fire?', I said me. He said I'd made it easy for him, and I had, deliberately. But I couldn't say that on TV and I wasn't going to spoil my grandson's trip to Brazil for anything.

Then there was the 'celebrity' game-playing going on in the background. It was obvious from the start that some people were trying to paint themselves into the best possible position, but at my age, I'm not interested in a celebrity profile. In fact, I never have been. It did disappoint me that Stephanie Rice sometimes didn't show respect for the rest of the team, and I told her that on the show, saying that if she were my daughter, I would put her over my knee and smack her backside! I also pulled her up on her communication skills with our driver and the rest of the crew. One example of Stephanie's comments was when she told Kyle and Jackie O on morning radio that I was 'jealous' of the money that the younger swimmers have today. I would have thought she knew enough about me and my story not to have disrespected me so publicly.

On another occasion during the shoot, some friends of mine flew in from London. They arrived in town at 10pm and were in Sydney for one night only. As I finished shooting at 10.30pm, I said I would meet them for a late supper. We had dinner and a glass of wine at Star Casino, and when they asked if I wanted to go and play some blackjack with them, I said, 'Sure, why not?'

We had a couple more wines and my friend gave me $1,000 to play blackjack for him. Well, I turned that $1,000 into $4,500 – I can't say that always happens – and went back to my room happy.

After a good sleep, I went straight into makeup the next morning, ready for the show. When the young makeup artist asked how my night was, I said I'd had a great time meeting up with friends from London, drinking a couple of wines and winning some money, but that I was tired after getting to bed about 1.30am. We all laughed. Stephanie, though, overheard the conversation and interpreted it as an all-night bender, and a regular occurrence to boot! Heavens above, I'm 75 years of age – imagine doing that every night for six weeks! I know I'm good, but I'm not that good. As a former publican, I also know how to have a drink and enjoy myself without overdoing it, yet Stephanie told Melbourne Radio and Kyle and Jackie O in Sydney: 'I don't know how (Fraser) does it ... she turned up some days after staying out all night ... and here I am needing my seven hours ... We were staying at The Star while we were filming, and so it was perfect, she was there on the pokies, doing the blackjack, a few drinks and then just straight into hair and makeup.'

Prue MacSween and I used to be on friendly terms, so I don't know what her problem was with me on the show. She was too foul-mouthed for my liking and I couldn't be bothered talking to her in the end. Prue and Roxy didn't get along because they have rival PR companies, but I liked Roxy straight away. She's dynamic, she knows what she wants, and that's why she's been so successful in business. If she said she was going to do something, she did it then and there. When we had the dry cleaning challenge and Jeff Fenech stole the charger from the camera, Roxy just rang her office and got another one sent over – problem solved. We won the challenge and $100,000.

At the end of the show, I won $40,000 for my charity, and

I was very happy with that. Mark Bouris was a real gentleman and I appreciated his 'gentle' firing. I enjoyed the show overall; the production team gave us good feedback and told us truthfully how we were going.

Something that did disappoint me was the number of people I asked to support my charity challenge and heard nothing back from. I'm talking about some high profile, successful people, who didn't even return my calls. After raising a couple of thousand dollars here and there, my old mate John 'Singo' Singleton was the one to put up serious money, which says volumes about him. Times are tough, I know, so the response probably says a lot about the state of the economy at the moment. But I didn't raise nearly as much money as I wanted and it shook my boots a little bit. People are hanging on to what they have and not sharing it around where it's needed, the bottom line being that they don't want to get involved – they're 'money rich' and 'time poor'.

I gave it my best shot and some of the youngsters a run for their money, I think. I was out shopping recently and a mother stopped to say hello with her two children. 'Well done on *Celebrity Apprentice*,' she said. 'We thought you were fantastic. You should have won.'

I told her I enjoyed myself and thanked her for her support.

'How did you keep your cool?' she asked me.

'There were times there when I didn't.'

'Well, you were a great representative for people like us … ordinary people,' she said.

Mission accomplished.

chapter 2

Know the worth of hard work

There's an old saying that you don't know who you are unless you know where you come from.

My father Kenneth Fraser was a Scot. He came to Australia before World War I and worked as a shipwright aboard the *Queen Mary*, which was used as a hospital ship during the war. Pop, as I called him, settled in Balmain, Sydney, after the war, where he met my mother, Rose Miranda, at a local soccer match. Her family originally came from Peru, but I didn't find that out until I was much older. I still don't even know what year Mum was born. I do know that she was in her forties when she had me, the youngest of her nine children (eight of whom survived birth). The older kids were Ken Jr, Rose Jr, Heather, Joyce and John, while the younger three were Alick, Donnie and me. I was born on 4 September 1937 in Balmain.

We were a working class family. My father worked at nearby Cockatoo Island, while Mum looked after us and took on odd jobs. We rented a terrace in Birchgrove, and while we never had much, we never went without. It was a typically inner-city Australian upbringing.

I told them I would buy the house for them one day. And I did.

Dad taught us the importance of work, as Mum and Dad strove very hard to support our family. I'd come home from school and see 48 men's work shirts hanging on the line. In those days, there were no washing machines, so they were all washed by hand in the tub and scrubbed on a washboard, and then Mum would starch and iron them when they were dry – all to feed us. We'd run messages around the neighbourhood, and might get a halfpenny for it, but you'd be surprised how all those halfpennies added up. All the money we earned went into the communal money jar for Mum. The odd time I came home with a bag full of lollies instead of the penny, I would cop it from my brothers Alick and Donnie.

I can remember my pop making a wheelbarrow for me, so I could do the produce run for the neighbours on a Saturday morning; I used to deliver goods to local pensioners who weren't able to get up to the shops and markets. I also had a paper run at the Manly Wharf, which was fantastic of a Saturday afternoon, with so many people coming back from the races. The papers cost tuppence, but people would give you threepence and tell you to keep the change. When the papers went to threepence, you rarely got a tip, although some would pay sixpence and give you a threepence tip, especially if they'd won at the races. Mum had bought me a fob coat with four pockets in it and I used it like a cash register – halfpennies go here, pennies in there, threepences and sixpences in the other pockets. At the end of the day, I'd sit down and work out how many papers I'd sold and how much profit I'd made. Sometimes I'd come home with as much as £3, which was a lot of money in those days.

It was a very healthy lesson I learned from my parents – to work hard and to be honest – and I hope I have taught my daughter and grandson the same.

I very quickly understood the value of money and how hard you have to work for it. I still remember, as a little girl during the war years, standing in queues with food coupons in my hand and not allowing anybody to take those coupons from me. I'd be lining up for bread, butter, eggs, bacon – food that was so important to our family. Although I was only six years old, when some of the adults tried to grab the coupons out of my hand, I'd kick them in the shins or bite their hands so they couldn't get them. Most people my age remember what it's like to have lived through the effects of the Great Depression and the World War, and I think that really steeled our generation.

Although I was the youngest, I was often allowed to sit up at night and listen to the adults talk about the war; I remember my uncles sitting around the kitchen table in their army uniforms. When we had air raids, we were frightened, but we had the adults there to look after us. They'd put their arms around us and say, 'This is what we're fighting for.' You grew up respecting that.

I loved growing up in a working class suburb, where I learned discipline, respect for my elders and self-respect. I also grew up in an era when a smack on the backside was worth a thousand words, but was always administered with love. I had beautiful parents – they sometimes made decisions that I didn't agree with, but they loved me unconditionally and wanted the best for me. They certainly taught me right from wrong.

As a family, we talked about everything, with the evening meal being a time for coming together. My mother only cooked one main meal a day, so we would all sit down at the table for dinner, with Pop at the head. We would have to make sure we had clean hands, clean nails and clean ears, because we used to play in the coal mine.

As a child, my first love was horses, although it was too expensive a pastime for a working-class family like ours. I couldn't have afforded to care for my own horse, or pay for feed and riding boots and lessons, but my friends and I used to care for the council horses stabled in paddocks along the Parramatta River, riding them up to the Lane Cove National Park for exercise on the weekends. There was not a lot of traffic, so we could cut through the bush and vacant land. I have tried to be near horses all my life.

Of course, the other great passion I developed was a love of the water. I used to go with my brothers and my friends to the Balmain Baths in Elkington Park, the oldest saltwater harbour pool and swimming club in Australia, and we'd be there all day. We spent so much time at Balmain Baths we thought we owned the place, and thirty years later, they renamed the pool the Dawn Fraser Baths – what an honour! We also had picnics at other tidal baths that had nets down to protect people from sharks, like Manly, Nielsen Park, Picnic Point and Greenwich. It was part of growing up in Australia, making our own fun, swimming and diving off the springboards, playing water polo and lazing in the sun.

I was a tomboy, and pretty wild as far as swimming was concerned, but I joined the Leichhardt/Balmain League of Swimmers because I suffered from asthma and the exercise was good for me. Along with my brothers Alick and Donnie, I started to train under the watchful eye of my uncle, Ray 'Chut' Miranda, and developed a real affinity for the water … and for racing. When I was nine years old, the League took a squad of swimmers to Broken Hill to swim in a meet. I don't remember anything about the races I swam in, but I have vivid memories of the trip there. We travelled by train and stayed up all night playing cards for money, as we didn't have sleepers – nine years of age and playing cards for cash! I won all my pocket money for the week, playing cards. These are the things you never forget – your personal history, the stories of growing up.

Even though I was part of a strong family unit, I also had an independent spirit. We had the run of the streets, because there was no traffic to speak of, only the odd horse and cart, so we could play rounders or cricket in the middle of the road. On weekends, we'd put a fire under the copper, because my brothers' football mates would be back for a beer and Mum would wash their jerseys.

My brothers Alick and Donnie gave me a lot of support and the three of us were very close. They looked after me and took me everywhere – to football, the baths, the movies, concerts and fireworks. Both were talented athletes in their own right and took great delight in showing off their diving skills at Balmain Baths. I used to climb up on their backs and drop 30 feet to the water below, knowing my brothers were in control. Donnie had the hardest feet in the world; he rarely wore shoes because Mum and Dad couldn't afford them. I can still remember him carrying me across the hot bitumen schoolyard, and later, he would stand on blocks of ice in his job as an ice deliveryman. I admired Donnie so much ... he was my hero.

When I was about 14, Donnie was playing rugby league for the famous Codocks Club, in the junior rugby league competition. When he came back to our house with his football mates that afternoon, as he always did, he was bleeding from the mouth and it wouldn't stop. He'd had two wisdom teeth out that week, so we thought it might have been that, but the bleeding got worse and he started frothing at the mouth. He was rushed to Balmain Hospital, where he was diagnosed with leukemia.

Not much was known about the disease at the time and we certainly didn't talk about it. Donnie had his 21st birthday in hospital and died two weeks later. Dad wouldn't allow me to go to the funeral, but I stood on the porch of the Bridge Hotel as a police escort led the funeral car past the Balmain Leagues Club. Alick and his football mates, all wearing their team blazers, formed a guard of honour down Victoria Road.

Some people today wouldn't understand, but that was how it was handled in those days; children never went to funerals.

At around the same time, a local swimming coach named Harry Gallagher had begun to notice my swimming ability at Balmain Baths, and wanted me to join his squad at Drummoyne. Donnie had always encouraged me to train hard and do my best. He always believed in me, even though I was just a little girl.

My beautiful brother became my inspiration.

chapter 3

Love what you do

WHEN SCHOOLCHILDREN ARE DOING PROJECTS ON FAMOUS AUSTRALIANS, SUCCESSFUL SPORTSPEOPLE OR THE OLYMPIC GAMES, THEY'LL OFTEN WRITE TO ME. 'I have to do a project on a famous Australian and I chose you,' they say. 'These are the 10 questions I would like to ask you.'

Most of the time, the questions are the same – they want to know about swimming, and how a young girl's talent took her round the world. So here are those top 10 questions for you, along with the short answers.

Was swimming always your dream or did you plan to have another career?
No, swimming wasn't my first choice, I planned to be a doctor.

Why did you choose swimming?
I did it because I had very bad asthma and the sport was cheap. I only needed a costume and towel ... my family couldn't afford much.

Was swimming your first choice of sports?
No. My first love was horses, but horseriding was just too expensive.

What made you want to be a great swimmer?
I was an asthmatic and knew swimming was good for my health.

What swimming clubs did you swim for?
Leichhardt/Balmain, Balmain Ladies Amateur Swimming Club & Crystal Pool Amateur Swimming Club (Adelaide), Melbourne Olympic Amateur Swimming Club (Melbourne).

Who were your swimming coaches?
'Chut' Miranda for the first few years, then Harry Gallagher took over for the rest of my swimming career.

Why did you get banned in 1964?
I marched in the opening ceremony when I wasn't supposed to, and wore an unofficial swimsuit in some of the races.

Who do you look up to?
My brother Donnie.

Do you swim anymore?
Yes, although not a lot. I like to take my grandson swimming.

How do you feel about your success?
I feel good about what I achieved, because I trained and worked very hard to become the best at what I did.

You have to fall in love with your sport, I tell them, because it gets harder rather than easier. If you love what you do, you have a better chance at being successful.

In the early 1950s, Harry Gallagher ran Drummoyne Swimming Pool, and trained an elite bunch of young swimmers to great success. He had a champion swimming squad that included Jon Henricks, who later won the gold medal at Melbourne for the men's 100m freestyle. When the pool was shut down for renovations, he needed another place to train his squad and Leichhardt Council said he could use our stomping ground, Balmain Baths.

I resented these outsiders coming to our pool. Our gang used to jump off the diving platform and bomb them. 'Watch out for the eels and the sharks!' we teased.

'Who's the girl over there?' Harry asked someone at the Baths one day.

'That's Dawn Fraser,' he was told.

'Does she swim?'

I had been a member of the Leichhardt/Balmain League of Swimmers since I was a kid, and some of my friends and brothers were too. It was all very social on weekends, racing and lazing around the pool. I loved it, even though I suffered sinus, ear and eye trouble from the chlorine. The adults would put industrial-strength grease in my ears to stop the water getting in, but the pain after a meet was sometimes unbearable.

'Want to have a race with these kids?' Harry asked me when I was about 13, referring to the Drummoyne swimmers. The baths at Balmain were 73⅓ yards long and the council had put a pontoon on one end to make it a 55-yard start. Jon Henricks was standing there, ready to race, and I was standing at the corner of the pontoon, about 20 yards in front of him.

'Why would I want to race him for?' I shrugged. I was interested, but I didn't want to show him that.

Ricksy, who later became a firm friend, shot out the challenge, 'I bet you can't beat me.'

'Why would I want to?' I replied. The words had barely left my mouth when I had dived in and started swimming for my life. I had about 20 metres start on Ricksy, but he just caught me.

Harry then asked if I'd like to train with his squad. 'No,' I told him, 'I don't want to swim because training is boring, going up and down the pool all the time.' If he'd wanted me to train jumping off the tower, I was up for that!

But over the summer, Harry persisted in asking me. 'I want to come and talk to your mother and father about training with my swim squad,' he asked eventually. 'Where do you live?'

I was having none of that. 'I'm not telling you,' I said, before adding, 'and my Mum and Pop told me not to talk to strangers.' Looking back on it today, my God, I was cheeky!

It was late one afternoon when I hopped on my bike to ride home from the pool and found Harry waiting in his convertible. 'You should get a light for that bike,' he said.

I told him he should mind his own bloody business and rode home, with Harry following all the way.

'I want to call on your mother and father,' he said, as we pulled up outside my house.

'They won't talk to you,' I told him.

But he came back the next night anyway and knocked on our door. 'I'm Mr Harry Gallagher, the swimming coach from Drummoyne,' he told Pop when he was invited inside. 'And I'd like to train Dawn.'

'Only if Dawn wants to,' Pop replied.

Deep down, I wanted badly to train with Harry. He was a very charismatic coach and I liked what he was doing with the other kids. I knew he could improve me as swimmer too. So I said yes, and after that, I was determined to prove to Mum and Dad that they were right to allow me to focus on swimming.

What did Mr Gallagher see in me? A bit of raw talent, I think, plus the strength of my stroke in the water – thanks to all those years pushing my wheelbarrow up the street! I'm also a 'straight arm shooter'; coaches always said I needed to bend my arm under the water, but I kept my arm straight. Even today, I'm very strong in the forearms.

As I began to train, I started to 'feel' the water and really enjoy it. Not that it was all plain sailing, of course. I gave Harry a hard time at first, rebelling against his disciplined routines; in particular, I'd be annoyed when I wanted a day off and he wouldn't give it to me. At other times, when I didn't do what he asked in training, he would tell me to get out of the pool and I would stand in the change rooms with a cigarette hanging out of my mouth, just to provoke him. He'd calmly say, 'Put that thing out.' He should have let me smoke it, then watched me cough my lungs up after a couple of laps, but that wasn't his style either. He knew how to give me a little bit of headway, and exactly how and when to rein me in.

Harry's routine taught me to develop the discipline to get up early in the morning and train. He motivated me to aim for what I wanted to achieve, not what he wanted to achieve. He knew he could help me reach my best, but it was always on my agenda, not his. All the while, I desperately wanted to prove myself to him. I was often called a lazy trainer in my career, but that just wasn't the case – I wouldn't have broken 41 world records if it was!

Swimming is a lonely sport, but the water became the love of my life. I loved the solitude of it, getting in the 'zone', lap after lap. Now when I get into the water after not having swum for a while, it all comes back to me. I find myself floating on top, embracing it. Some people swim too low – they're too rigid and they don't want to put their faces in. But the more you practise, the more you float. The water will make a path for you, believe me.

It concerns me that learning to swim is not a huge priority for some families today. Maybe they don't see the value in teaching their kids to swim – or they just don't have the time – but Australia is an island surrounded by water! Wherever you go there are beaches, swimming pools, rivers, creeks and dams. You *have* to learn to swim, for safety if nothing else.

My grandson went swimming with his mother at Coogee Beach in Sydney last Christmas. She lost hold of him at one point and he got dumped in a wave. They were swimming between the flags, but for a moment she couldn't find him in the water. Eventually she saw the top of his head as he floated by and managed to pull him out. When they came home, they looked like they'd stepped out of the desert, all covered in sand. It was a scary situation, and it's been very hard to get him back in the water, but we'll get there. He'll be even more confident when he starts swim school.

In the 1980s, when I was in my late forties, I was asked to join the Masters Games movement by my friend Les Martins, President of the Australian Weightlifting Federation. Masters Swimming was set up to 'encourage all adults, regardless of ability, to swim regularly and compete in order to promote fitness and improve their general wellbeing'. I wanted to keep swimming to be fit and healthy, but I also didn't want to feel like I was getting old, I guess. The inaugural Masters Games were held in Toronto, Canada, in 1985, and the women I swam against were very competitive. They took it very seriously and I got the distinct impression that they wanted to beat Dawn Fraser!

In the end I thought, *Bugger this, I'm not going to be beaten by these ladies*, and it didn't take me long to get me back into the competitive mindset. Once you have it, I think you always have it. I competed in the 45–49 years age group and I won the

100m in 69.8 seconds. The media attention was overwhelming. Not only was it great to be swimming for Australia again, but I was also a 47-year-old veteran.

The next year I attended the Masters Games in Tokyo, and although I picked up another gold and five silvers, I was beaten for the first time in a 100m race. And you know what? I felt fine about that too. It was as if I had moved on in my life. It was about being fit and healthy and able to compete, not just winning, and I've enjoyed competing in many Masters Games in the decades since. I also became the patron of the Centralian Masters Games in Alice Springs in 1986, the first Masters to be held in Australia. I competed in these every two years until the mid-1990s.

I don't swim competitively anymore, since I tore the bursa in my shoulder – a thin sac of tissue in between the muscles in the shoulder and hip – in a fall a couple of years ago. I want to get back swimming, and my grandson needs to swim too, because he's asthmatic like me. If I got enough training under my belt, I would love to have a swim at Alice Springs again.

I suppose I'm just one of those people – and this is what my coaches taught me – who has to train for an event if I want to win it. I know I can't just jump in the pool and expect to be competitive. I've done that before, and it hurts not to succeed.

chapter 4

Never stop learning

As I grew into an awkward adolescent in the mid-1950s, I left school at age 14 to start learning a trade. I trained as a dressmaker with the Larco factory where my sister Joyce worked and was also throwing myself into training with Harry Gallagher. I loved getting up at 4am and riding my bike to Drummoyne every morning. After training, I would stay and work in the shop for an hour, then ride back to work. I had started to make a name for myself in amateur swimming, and although I was a terror to train at times, Harry was educating me and teaching me self-discipline.

Then, in 1955, Coach was given the lease on a pool in Adelaide and said he was heading interstate.

Being young – just 17 – my first concern was for myself. How was I going to train? How was I going to improve in competition? Melbourne was hosting the Olympics the following year, and that had been our goal.

'Would you like me to ask your father if you could come to Adelaide and continue training?' Harry asked.

'Pop wouldn't let me,' I told him. I knew my parents wouldn't allow me to leave home before the age of 21, so the idea of moving to Adelaide – and with a man, even it was my coach! – was out of the question. But Harry offered to talk to Pop anyway. He came over to the house for dinner one night, and finally broached the subject (although I had to kick him under the table a bit to get the conversation going).

'I've got a good job in South Australia,' he began, 'with the lease of a pool for five years.'

Pop piped up straight away. 'You don't have to ask me, she's not going. You know my rule, she can't leave home before 21 years of age.'

'Pop,' I said, 'I really would like to go. I did everything right and trained hard. I represented Mr Gallagher and the club at district and state finals and I've done very well there and been very good, never had a bad report. Just give me the chance. I'd really like to do it.'

He said he would think about it.

The next time the subject came up, he asked if I'd be working in Adelaide, and I told him yes – I'd already applied for a job and would make sure I sent money home to Mum. I had it all organised. Harry was driving to Adelaide with his mother, so I could travel with them, with Harry's mum acting as a 'chaperone' along the way. The two of us would stay together in one motel, Harry in another. Harry also suggested I get my learner's permit and drive part of the way there, then get my full licence in Adelaide, but that didn't go down well with Pop!

Finally, my father gave me an ultimatum. 'Dawnie, it's now July,' he said. 'Championships are in February next year. You can go, but if you haven't improved your time by two seconds by February, you have to come back home.'

I promised I would improve, and I did – I bettered my time by five seconds and broke the world record, which set me up for success in the 1956 Olympics.

Adelaide was a great environment for training. Starting in August, I got up at 4am every morning, which meant I had the pool to myself. It was too cold to put my head under – there were no heated pools in those days and Adelaide is very cold in winter – so I used to start with kicking, holding on to a board. Come September, I could at least put my face in the water. I'd get out and do callisthenics, and also did a bit of running and weight training. I was tall for my age at five-foot-nine, slim with broad shoulders.

A professor from Sydney University had invented an electro-cardiograph machine and came to Adelaide to test it on me, on Harry's invitation. After I finished a session, he'd measure my performance on the machine. It was all very unusual and cutting-edge, not unlike the work triathletes do today, but I never once doubted my coach. If Harry said, 'Go over to the pullies and do a set of 1,000,' I would have gone and done it.

In the back of mind, there was always Pop's ultimatum: I had to improve my time by two seconds.

In Adelaide, I became more independent. Harry and his mother lived at the pool and I had the flat above their quarters. I did my own washing and ironing and Mrs Gallagher would cook breakfast for us all. I got a job as an assistant sportswear buyer at the Charles Birks department store; my boss hated me turning up to work with wet hair. I also got a second job working Thursday, Friday and Saturday nights in a coffee lounge. On weekends, I pumped petrol and did some 'water work' for the famous horse trainer Colin Hayes, grooming and hosing down the horses and taking them to the beach for a swim. Any money I earned was put away to pay for a flight home to Sydney in case of emergency. The airfare would have been about £50 to £60, a lot of money in the 1950s. I also sent some to Mum each week, as all my brothers and sisters had done. A phone call home cost up to £2, so if I wanted to talk to Mum and Dad, I had to budget for it.

I thought independently and acted independently, but I achieved what I did because I always had my family in my corner, and I didn't want to fail them. I got homesick, sure. I even went home early at one point. But Pop encouraged me to go back, as I hadn't finished the job I had gone there to do.

Harry ultimately trimmed his squad to six swimmers, and when the Nationals came round in February 1956, I broke the world record.

Dale Krieg and I became very good friends in Adelaide. Dale was a member of the squad Harry prepared for the Olympics, and when I wasn't working, I spent most of my weekends at Dale's house at West Beach, waterskiing and swimming. Her father was a pilot for TAA, and occasionally, if Captain Krieg was flying from Adelaide to Sydney, he would tell the authorities I was his daughter and fly me home for free. Dale and I looked alike, so we got away with it, not to mention a lot of other mischief.

My first experience of an indoor training pool was when we went to Broken Hill in 1956 in the lead-up to the Olympics. The Zinc Company let us use their little 25-yard heated pool for a couple of months, and it was absolutely fantastic training in the wintertime in a warm pool. We also got plenty of attention from the local miners. They actually allowed me to go down into the mines once, an unheard-of thing at the time, and I wasn't allowed to say anything about it. I still occasionally get letters from people who live out there, asking if remember swimming at Broken Hill.

Ahead of the 1956 Olympics, there wasn't much pressure from the media, because we were all new kids on the block. They knew who we were, but we hadn't done anything yet. There were reporters in Melbourne, like Ken Knox, who were the main writers for the swimmers but there was nothing really controversial in those days and they didn't focus on personal issues. None of that came in until much later. And Harry wasn't the type of coach to hype us up, either. His main focus was to get his swimmers trained and ready to compete.

I lived in Adelaide for six years altogether, from 1955 to 1961. It was a world away from what I was used to, but I liked the history of Adelaide. Living there fulfilled my desire to learn more about life, and especially about my country. After the 1956 Olympics, I was invited to lots of country areas and I met fascinating people who taught me so much. I was invited to Anne Kidman's family home in Eringa – she trained at our pool and we'd become firm friends – where I heard many stories of outback Australia. Anne was a descendant of the original Kidman cattle baron, so her family knew all about bush history. Kym Bonython, a neighbour of the Kriegs' at West Beach, taught me about art, and I watched Albert Namitjira paint. I met Sir Robert Helpmann, who invited me to the ballet at the Theatre Royal, and I had morning tea with Sir Robert George, the Governor of South Australia, and his wife. Windy Hill-Smith, a horse breeder I met through Colin Hayes, invited me to his vineyards and taught me all about wine.

And of course, there was Harry Gallagher, my coach, mentor and friend, who fostered my love of art and jazz and turned me into a world champion.

Along with these amazing experiences, I still had to juggle work commitments and my swimming career. After my success at the Melbourne Olympics, the managing director of the Charles Birk department store, Mr Norman George, asked me what I wanted to do with my life. Did I see my future as an assistant sportswear buyer or in swimming? I told him I wanted to swim for Australia, but the reality was that I needed to work to support myself. As I saw it, this was a job I could do after I gave up swimming, but I didn't know when that was going to be. No one in Australia had long sports careers at the time, because they couldn't afford it. It was usually one big hit – representing Australia at an Olympics. I certainly didn't envisage that I would still be competing at the Tokyo Olympics eight years after the 1956 Games.

Mr George asked how often I trained and I told him every day. He respected the fact that I was working so hard to make ends meet and offered to transfer me to the bulk store, to work with Mr Rumsby. 'What am I going to do out there?' I asked.

'I'll arrange that you come in when you finish your training,' he said. 'If it's 8am, that's fine, because they open at 7am. You can train during your lunch hour too. Start your break at 12pm, be down the pool by 12.15pm and back at work by 1.00 pm.'

He also said I could finish work at 3pm in the afternoon and he'd pay me a full wage, or if I got the invoices processed by 12pm and worked through my lunch break, I could finish for the day.

It was quite an opportunity. I talked to Coach about it, and he said we could do three sessions a day.

Around this time, I also opened a swimming pool for George Bolton ,who was the mayor of an Adelaide suburb. He asked how he could pay me for the services, but I explained I couldn't take money due to my amateur status. George then asked me how I got to work each day, and I told him I caught the bus or walked. I had a licence but I couldn't afford a car.

'Can you ride a push bike?' he asked.

'Yeah,' I said.

'How about a motorbike, then?' he offered – George owned a motorcycle store. I wasn't keen on the idea, so he suggested a scooter. He sold me a brand new Diana, the first motor scooter in Adelaide, and allowed me to pay off the £299 price tag at the rate of a pound a week. He registered it for me, serviced it for me and gave me the helmet.

It was a top-of-the-range machine. I even rode it from Adelaide to Sydney in the late 1950s with some friends. We came up through the Riverina, some of the nicest land I had ever seen. It took us three days in all and we slept beneath parked semi-trailers on the side of the road.

In my six-and-a-half years living in Adelaide, I tried to keep busy and enjoy as much of life as I could, which held some of my loneliness at bay. And I was lonely, without my parents, brothers and sisters. I used to do my training, eat my dinner, have a shower and go into my room to listen to jazz music or Rachmaninoff. I did a lot of thinking this way, contemplating what I wanted to do with my life, and exactly what I wanted to achieve.

chapter 5

When you're knocked down, get up again

I HAVE ALWAYS BEEN A REBEL, ESPECIALLY WHEN I WAS YOUNGER, AND THAT LARRIKIN SPIRIT HAS GOT ME INTO TROUBLE OVER THE YEARS. Swimming officials seemed to dislike me immediately, which I put down to my being outspoken, and coming from a working-class background. But I'm the sort of person who just knocks over any hurdles put in front of me. If I come crashing down to earth in the process, I just get right up.

I had joined the Leichhardt/Balmain League of Swimmers because my brothers swam there. The League was not affiliated with the Amateur Swimming Union because they were a social club. Their rules were that you had to be over the age of 16 to receive money for winning races, so the club would convert my race wins to points. At the end of the season, those points were added up and I would have enough money to buy myself a trophy, which I would receive on presentation night. I knew I wasn't allowed to receive a cash prize, but I would look around the local shops for a suitable trophy to buy.

When I was about 12, I saw a mantelpiece clock while I was shopping, which was worth a couple of pounds. I went back and told the committee I wanted to buy a clock for my parents with my trophy points. I don't know whether they added more money to my points or not, but on presentation night I was handed this lovely gift, which I proudly presented to my parents.

Then in 1951, I joined an amateur swim club, and was entered into the Western Suburbs championships at Enfield Baths. The club entered me in a 55-yard handicap race and had to submit my time, so they put down 33 seconds. The rule was I had to swim within two seconds of that time. Lorraine Crapp, a blonde, roly-poly girl from Cabarita, was the favourite for the race and her time was put down as 31 seconds. Lorraine was a year younger than me, but she was already the golden girl of junior swimming. She went on to set records from 110 to 880 yards, but to me, she was just a name in the program. I was given two seconds' start on Lorraine and I beat her – just.

My uncle 'Chut' Miranda was walking up and down the pool the whole time, screaming out, 'Come on, Dawnie! Come on!' Bill Berge Phillips, a Sydney solicitor and secretary of the Amateur Swimming Union (ASU) walked up to Chut and said, 'Who is that kid?'

'That's Dawn Fraser from Balmain,' Chut said proudly.

I had swum within my two seconds and Lorraine hadn't; I'd beaten her by a touch. At first the officials disqualified me because they said I had broken my two-second handicap, but Chut conferred with the timekeeper, who said I had swum 31.8 seconds. He protested and I was reinstated as winner.

After the meet, Uncle Chut and I were summoned to the ASU offices in North Sydney. There Bill Berge Phillips, sitting behind this big leather desk, thumped his hand down. 'You're a professional,' he said. 'You've been taking money from the Leichhardt/Balmain League.'

Phillips knew the club paid race winners a couple of shillings, but not that the club had bought my family a clock with my points. Chut said I hadn't taken any money, but Phillips would not listen. 'While I'm secretary, you will never swim for Australia,' he told me.

Swimming for Australia had not even entered my mind at that point – but it did then. I said, 'I will be that good, you will have to pick me.'

Chut took me by the hand and we left the room.

I had to stand down from competition for two years to regain my amateur status. When I was down the baths, I couldn't swim against any of the other kids, lest I ruin their amateur status too. It is a very lonely feeling knowing you have been excluded from something you love, and I was heartbroken. I continued training, while my uncle and Carol Mackintosh, a lovely lady from the Balmain Amateur Swimming Association, worked to get me reinstated. I finally was, after 18 months on the sidelines. It was the first of my many battles with the ASU.

Back then, the ASU was an Old Men's Club – there wasn't a woman on the Board – and I found their attitude, especially to us young girls, condescending. 'You will do what we say; we control you; we have your career in our hands; you belong to OUR association.'

I'm glad to say I didn't crumble under the pressure, even as a young teenager starting out, and I went out of my way to prove them wrong. I hadn't taken money, and once Bill Berge Phillips gave me a challenge, I knew I was going to succeed. I also think they were extra hard on me because I was from a working-class suburb, and nothing has swayed me from that thought in the decades since. They wanted meek and mild swimmers, but I spoke my mind, as my mother and father taught me to do.

Later, I proved Phillips wrong by competing at the Melbourne Olympics, but I remember him telling the squad that he didn't expect any of the female swimmers to back up for the Rome Olympics in four years time because there was a new generation of swimmers ready to take our place. He probably thought he'd seen the end of me!

I actively fought the ASU to get rid of their amateur status. After the Melbourne Olympics, if I was invited to do a TV show, I would be given £20 appearance money. That was to cover taxi fare to and from the studio, getting my hair done, and buying new stockings and a decent outfit. I would have to account for every cent – that's why I hate doing receipts to this day – but I always did get those payments verified. Perhaps the ASU didn't realise that I had been taught to budget from an early age.

When I returned to Australia after capturing a gold medal at the 1960 Rome Olympics, I was effectively banned again for 12 months – officially because I refused to swim the butterfly leg in a heat of the 4 x 100 medley relay, which apparently embarrassed swimming officials and 'upset' swimmer Jan Andrews. The ASU claimed it had cost her a silver medal. I had also 'refused' to wear the Australian tracksuit, had taken part in an 'unauthorised exhibition' swim in Switzerland after the Games, and was the subject of a poor manager's report about my socialising in Rome. This felt really unfair. I knew how to enjoy myself, and I knew where to draw the line, not to mention that other athletes had enjoyed themselves too – they just didn't have the name 'D. Fraser'. It did seem that the ASU were looking for reasons to ban me in the end. Bill Berge Phillips told the press that there were 'bigger issues' behind my ban, which they should try and find out.

From my perspective, it seemed like tall poppy syndrome at its worse. I'm a naturally gregarious person, and swimming gave me the opportunity to meet many interesting people around the world, some of whom I'm still friends with today. I was being invited to functions and entertained in high circles, but the swimming officials weren't. I was of age, acting like a normal 22-year-old, and my mother and father knew what I was doing. I wasn't bringing undue stress on them and I was doing my job in the pool, representing my country at a very important event.

When I was left out of the Australian team in the 12 months after the Rome Olympics, I felt like giving up swimming. I was keen to move to Melbourne – I'd had enough of living on my own in Adelaide and wanted to be closer to friends and explore new job opportunities. I also felt that Harry wasn't supporting me in my battles with the ASU, because he wasn't part of the Australian coaching squad, and we decided to split for a while. Before long, though, we reconnected when Harry came to Melbourne for work and set a new goal of making my third Olympics Games.

Next came the biggest shock of all – the ASU's decision to ban me for 10 years. The reasons were two-fold: one, I had disobeyed the ASU and the manager's instruction not to march in the opening ceremony; and two, I had disobeyed the ASU and the manager and worn an unofficial swimsuit in one of the events. Ten years for those two indiscretions, which were fully explained at the time to the managers in charge of the team.

The ban was described as 'harsh' and 'oppressive' by a press contingent who hadn't always been on my side, although *The Sun* journalist Ernie Christensen was fed libelous information from Bill Berge Phillips, which he was silly enough to print (and for which I successfully sued). Some reported that my ban was due to an infamous incident with the Olympic flag in Tokyo, but that wasn't the case.

I was able to challenge the ASU ban and win because I assembled a champion team in my defence – solicitor Ted France, Chief Justice Leslie Herron and famed jurist Sir Clive Evatt – but it ultimately cost me my swimming career.

Events in my life, time and time again, have forced me to be resilient and tough. I had to be, otherwise I might have locked myself away and cried all day. It's also part of my nature. When I was little, I was often knocked down by older siblings, but I quickly learned to just pick myself up. I used that resolve in my later life to face down the obstacles put up by officialdom.

As Roger Franklin noted in *The Age* in the 1970s, 'The Dawn Fraser case is often quoted as a prime example of the way sporting authorities can be their own worst enemies. Quite apart from alienating the public and giving authorities a poor reputation for mercy and common sense, it has helped create an impression of officials as order-shouting tin gods.'

When I was working as an Olympic Ambassador in the 1980s and 1990s, it was quite satisfying to run into members of the Australian Swimming Union and to be honoured with awards at the end of the 20th century. All those old men are dead now, but I knew it used to rile Berge Phillips when my name was announced. He disliked me to the end and I'm afraid there was no reconciliation between us.

chapter 6

Embrace your rivals

ALL OF AUSTRALIA EXPERIENCED SOMETHING SPECIAL WHEN MELBOURNE HOSTED THE 1956 SUMMER OLYMPICS. I doubt many Australian Olympic teams – not even the Sydney team in 2000 – experienced the same mateship we had in Melbourne.

The boys generally trained in a different swimming pool to the girls, and when we trained at the Melbourne Olympic Pool, we each had our own coaches there – Harry Gallagher, Sam Herford, Forbes Carlisle and Frank Guthrie. Those four coaches had no connection in the Australian team. They worked individually with swimmers and were not employed by the ASU.

Yet the competition generated by them was just what we needed. Lorraine Crapp wanted to beat me; Faith Leech wanted to beat both of us; and Sandra Morgan wanted to get into the relay team, so she beat the others. That's why Australia had the best relay team. We didn't have physiotherapists, mentors and specialist coaches like they do today. When our swimmers failed to do well in the 2012 Games in London, the coaches said they hadn't had enough international competition; in 1956, we didn't have any international competition, and we were still the best team ever! We were also at home and we never had that luxury again – not in Rome or in Tokyo, because our coaches did not travel with the team. As a result, we were never quite able to recapture the highs of that summer in 1956, when we won eight of thirteen swimming gold medals.

We were very competitive when we went into camp and trained in Townsville, Queensland, before the Games. We all used to sit up on the balcony, watching our rivals' workouts and training times, then report back to our coaches. At that stage, we were only a squad – we weren't even the Australian team – and we could have been dropped at any time. That meant one bad performance, or one bad week, and you would be out of the Olympics. It made everyone work very hard.

But Melbourne also proved that we could be competitive and still be supportive of each other, as we had great camaraderie at the Melbourne Olympics. I had been friends with Jon Henricks for years; when we met as kids at Balmain Baths, he was the first person I ever raced. We loved the cheekiness in each other, and still keep in contact now. After the Olympics, he went to the United States on a university scholarship and married a lovely American girl named Bonnie. During the Games, 'Ricksy' won the 100m gold medal, and I made it a sprint double when I won the 100m women's freestyle. He was also a member of the 4 x 200m gold medal-winning relay team, which included John Devitt, Kevin O'Halloran and Murray Rose.

Murray Rose was a beautiful man. He won three gold medals in Melbourne – the 400m and 1500m double, as well as the 4 x 200m relay. He also went to USC with Jon Henricks and formed a champion swim team with him. Murray came back in 1960, winning gold in the 400m and silver in the 1500m. He spent a long time in America, first as an actor and later as a broadcaster and journalist, before returning to Sydney to live with his second wife Jodi. He bravely battled leukemia in the final year of his life before passing away in 2012.

Lorraine Crapp and I were fierce rivals in the pool, but firm friends on dry land. We had been competitors since our teenage years and were still kids in many ways when the Olympics were held in 1956. Lorraine beat me in the 400m freestyle final and grabbed another gold when she joined me, Faith Leech and Sandra Morgan in the 4 x 100m freestyle relay. Lorraine later married Dr Bill Thurlow on the eve of the Rome Olympics, and they raised a family together. I'm still in contact with Faith and Sandra.

The swimmers didn't mix much with the athletics team in Melbourne, but I became good friends with Betty Cuthbert and Marlene Mathews, because they were my age. 'Cutho' was the golden girl of Australian athletics, winning gold in the 100m and 200m double, as well as the 4 x 100m relay. Marlene was terribly unlucky not to win gold, having grabbed bronze in the 100m and 200m behind Betty, and officials controversially left her out of the 4 x 100m relay team. Betty was injured in the Rome Olympics in 1960 and announced her retirement, but made a stunning comeback in Tokyo. She focused on the 400m, which was being run for the first time, and when she won gold, she became the only sprinter, male or female, to have won gold medals in all three events (100m, 200m and 400m). You can throw in the 4 x 100m relay as well!

'Cutho' hasn't been in great health in recent years, but she's a survivor, and she has a great family around her, including her twin sister, Marie. She lives in Western Australia and Rhonda, her carer, sends me a message every now and then to let me know how she's going. She just received a wonderful award in the UK that recognised her as one of the athletes of the century as an inaugural inductee of the IAAF (International Association of Athletics Federations) Hall of Fame.

As a team, we didn't realise how important the 1956 Olympics would be. We were the host nation, and the eyes of the world would be upon us, so a major-general was brought in from the Defence Corps to teach us how to march. The entire Australian team was put through marching drills. I can still remember the commander's voice underneath the stand, asking us to stand up and get ready to march. We were soon in line and shuffled up like we were in the forces. When we marched into the opening ceremony at the MCG, there was a roar from the crowd that I will never forget.

I was the world record holder for the 100m going into the Games, but Lorraine Crapp broke the record in the heat. I think she might have been the world record holder going into the final, because we were so close to one another, and the swimmer of the day was going to win the gold.

I can relive every stroke of that race in my mind, because it's something you never forget. We both got a good start and it was head to head. I think I got a better turn than her. I came out a little bit further and she drew up with me, but I was always renowned for my last 25 metres and that's where I won the race. It was such a close race that when I see the film, I can hear the announcer saying that neither of us knew who won; there was a touch in it. This was the era before electronic timing, so there were five judges behind each block comparing their times. I got the nod by 0.3 of a second. We were very fortunate that Australia had three swimmers in the 100m final – Lorraine, Faith Leech and myself – and that we finished 1, 2 and 3. In those days, teams could have three competitors in each event from each country, but today you're only allowed two, and you have qualifying times to make before you even get selected.

When I was racing with Lorraine, she wasn't a friend or a colleague, she was my competitor, but after beating her in the 100m, we came together as part of the relay team. We had six swimmers in our Olympic team in Melbourne, and Faith was the third in our relay team, but we could have had any one of the six as a fourth. In the end, Sandra Morgan won through in a swim-off with the others. The same four members had to swim the heats, semi-finals and the finals, while today you can pick eight swimmers in the relay. It's a recipe for disaster if you don't get the mix right. If anyone doesn't swim well in their heat, there may not be a semi-final or a final. The pay-off today, of course, is that if your team wins each member gets a medal whether they swam in the final or not.

We came together as a team and talked it over. We didn't even practise the changes for the relay – it was all just second nature to us. And we went out there and won the race. We had heats, semi-finals and finals back then (this format has recently been reintroduced to the Olympics, because they realised that heats and finals don't produce enough competition) and we had the whole swim team there supporting us. We also had the support of the Australian public.

In that era, women only had two distances, the 100m and the 400m, because officials viewed us as 'the weaker sex'. But my favourite length was 200m. The boys had the 4 x 200m relay and the 1,500m because they were 'the stronger sex'. I won the 100m in three successive Olympics, and I believe I could have done the same if there was a 200m freestyle event (the 200m was introduced in Mexico in 1968). I won the silver medal in the 400m freestyle event, although I hadn't trained for it. I was chosen to race because I was the second-fastest swimmer over that distance in Australia, but it was Lorraine Crapp's pet event. I gave it my best shot on the day, although my training up until then had been all sprint work. We learnt a lot from that experience, including how to train for two events.

At the end of the 1956 Olympics, Melbourne's *The Age* newspaper wrote, 'This was the most glorious week in the career of Dawn Fraser, and she reacted magnificently. As spokeswoman of the team, she faced large press and TV conferences repeatedly; she has had less formal education than most of her team-mates, but somehow it didn't show. She had poise and dignity, and she demonstrated an abundance of confidence without ever being cocky.'

If the men who ran the ASU read that, they took no notice of it.

chapter 7

Be humble, but hold your head up

AFTER THE MELBOURNE OLYMPICS, I WAS PUT ON A PEDESTAL, AND I FOUND IT VERY UNCOMFORTABLE TO BE IN THE PUBLIC EYE. I had become a household name overnight and had to cope with the attention as best I could. I never forgot where I had come from and who had helped me in my career – my coach Harry Gallagher, my family, my friends. Coach and I had our arguments at times of course (if you're spending as much time together as we did, you're bound to), but we always managed to mend our bridges.

In 1957, a group of us were invited to take part in the American Nationals in Houston, Texas. Lainey, 'Ricksy' and I swam in Honolulu, San Francisco, Ponca City in Oklahoma, where I swam the fastest 100 yards in history – 55.5 seconds – and finally in Houston. We stayed at the Hilton Hotel, where there was a pool in the shape of a grand piano. By the time I returned home, I had acquired a fake American accent and a big head!

After the Olympics, I had a scholarship offer from a university in San Francisco, but my father would not allow me to go and study in America because he felt it was just too far away. It was all right to live in Adelaide, because I could come home once a month, but if I studied in America I wouldn't be home for three years and that just wasn't on. My father was not going to allow our family to be separated.

While I understood and respected his decision, I was very upset at the time. I had matured in the three years since moving to Adelaide. My mind was aching for education and I wanted to learn how the rest of the world lived.

Years later, the University of Queensland offered me an honorary degree, but I knocked it back because I didn't think I was deserving of it. I had left school at fourteen-and-a-half and didn't even have an Intermediate Leaving Certificate. I now know that schooling is not all the education you can have. You can learn from the outside world too, and that's the education I received.

When I came back from America in 1957 and I had to use the outside toilet at my parents' house in the pouring rain, I complained, 'Why can't we have an inside loo like everyone else?' I had a fierce argument with my parents and said things in the heat of the moment that I really didn't mean – *up yours, I'm going, too good for this family, what have you given me?* Pop packed my bags the next morning and told me to get out of the house and go back to Adelaide if I wasn't happy. All of a sudden, I was sitting in a taxi thinking, 'Was it worth it? Losing your family over an outside toilet?'

When I arrived at the airport, I burst into tears. I got back in a taxi, went home and apologised.

I returned to Adelaide after my twentieth birthday and set my sights on the Nationals, and selection for the 1958 Commonwealth Games in Cardiff, Wales. I could see the younger girls coming up behind me; it was going to be a good team and I wanted to be part of it. Wales might also give me the opportunity to go to Scotland and see some of Dad's relatives. This goal gave me some time to settle down after the highs of my US trip and to plan the next phase of my career with Mr Gallagher. This was when Harry planted the seed that breaking the minute for the 100m was within my grasp. That achievement was still two years away, but it remained a major focus in my career.

At the Nationals in Melbourne, I won the 110 yards, beating Lorraine Crapp, and the 220 yards. I also won the 440 yards at the Nationals, and broke five minutes for the first time. Ilsa Konrads, who was only 14 at the time, finished second and Lainey was unplaced. I thought I might be named captain of the Australian swimming team for Cardiff, but was overlooked by the ASU, even though I was the oldest and best credentialled swimmer in the squad.

In Cardiff, I won gold in the 110 yards freestyle and 4 x 110 yards freestyle relay. Ilsa Konrads won the 440 yards race and I came second, but I was mainly concerned with maintaining my sprint crown and was happy for Ilsa. We also swam in the French Nationals and in Rotterdam as part of our European Tour, while the boys went to Japan. I bought a frock in Wales to wear to my 21st birthday, the week after I came back from Europe. My parents threw a party for me at the Chelmsford Hall. I think all of Balmain was there that night.

As I prepared for the Nationals in 1959 I started to feel unwell and was diagnosed with hepatitis. I lost my appetite, dropped a lot of weight and was advised not to swim in Hobart. My mother was coming down for the meet and the press had got a lot of mileage out of my anticipated clash with American Chris von Saltza. Against doctor's orders, I swam in the heats of the 110 and 220 yards, but withdrew from the 440 yards. I won the 110 yards race from Ilsa Konrads, with Chris back in third place, and on the last day of competition I beat Chris in the final of the 220 yards freestyle.

Even though I had overcome illness to win those events, some sections of the press labelled me a hypochondriac. This misconception was reinforced when I pulled out of the butterfly leg of the medley in Rome. I was actually allergic to the chlorine they used in the pools, and because we never wore goggles or ear plugs, it would play havoc with my sinus, ears and eyes through my whole career. On top of that, I was a chronic asthmatic, which didn't help my breathing in races.

At other times, I was accused in the press of being 'too masculine', as I was big and broad-shouldered and some of my times were faster than the male swimmers. As a young woman, that really gave my self-image a bit of a beating. Then there was the issue with my hair! I've always had short hair, ever since I was a little girl and my older brother cut my ponytail off so I could pass as a boy on his football team. Then as I developed as a swimmer, long hair wasn't an option because it weighed you down and affected your times, as well as getting in your mouth and eyes (this was before girls wore swimming caps). All the top swimmers wore their hair short. Jon Henricks even followed the overseas trend and started shaving his head in the late 1950s, but I wasn't going to go that far.

When I was invited to appear on television, hairdressers and makeup artists would try and do something with my hair, but there's not much they *could* do really; it has a mind of its own, because it's so thick. Even combing it makes it stick out!

When I was stood down for 12 months after the Rome Olympics in 1961, I couldn't escape the bad press. In Adelaide I was once arrested for 'loitering' when I was out on a date. We were stopped by a couple of policemen for speeding, but when I protested that they must have had us mixed up with another car because we had just pulled up to the coffee shop, they arrested me and took me to the city watchhouse. The police let me go that night after finding out who I was, saying it was all a misunderstanding, and the complaint was withdrawn. The local member for Norwood, future SA premier Don Dunston, even tabled the incident in the South Australian parliament and expressed his concern that something like that could happen in Adelaide. Premier Sir Thomas Playford stated that, 'South Australia should be very proud of Miss Dawn Fraser, who has been under considerable criticism outside the State.'

The criticism didn't stop, though. In August 1961, I discovered that someone from my club had entered me into the Victorian Winter championships, but hadn't mentioned it to me. The first I knew of it was when the papers reported 'a large crowd' had shown up to the Melbourne Olympic Pool to see me swim and been disappointed by my 'no show'. They said I should have issued an apology, but I hadn't even entered my name in the competition, and no one had ever asked me about my intention to compete!

Around this time, I decided to split with my coach Harry Gallagher and go to Melbourne to live, as I'd been offered a job there. I thought it was a good time to break away from Harry and strike out on my own. I worked at Myer, as well as co-ordinating seven different local sports, including teaching blind children to swim at Ashburton. I stayed with friends at Mt Eliza for a while before getting a small flat in Melbourne. My brother-in-law sent me a little German Shepherd pup, who I loved. I was very happy there ... and I also decided to start training again.

At first, I was swimming by myself at Melbourne Olympic Pool and Richmond Baths, but I was falling into lots of bad habits. I had no one to guide me and my heart wasn't in it. Then Harry came to Melbourne to take up a coaching position at Burwood, and we made up; I really was missing training under him. The Commonwealth Games were being held in Perth in 1962, so we decided to give it another shot together. He got me ready for the 1962 Nationals first, where I won the 110 and 440 yards double.

Before my father died at the end of 1961, he told me not to give up on my sport and not to let the officials know they had hurt me. At the Commonwealth Games in Perth in 1962, I like to think I did Pop proud, winning gold in the 110 and 440 yards freestyle, as well as playing my part in the 4 x 110 and 4 x 440 yard relays.

I also had the new challenge Harry had set me – breaking the minute mark for the 100m.

I decided not to go to Townsville with the Australian squad before the Perth Games, because I couldn't afford it. Harry had decided not to coach Australia too, because the ASU had arranged for the men and women to train in different towns, about 8 miles apart. This was probably for 'propriety' reasons, but would have made things impossible for Harry to manage, and it was not how Harry had ever trained me – he thought working the boys and girls together was good for competition.

When we got to the Commonwealth Games trials in Melbourne in October 1962, I knew I hadn't missed out on anything. I would even say I was fitter than my competitors after training solo under Harry's watchful eye. I became the first person to break the minute mark when I recorded 59.9 seconds for the 100m. A month later, I swam a new record of 59.5 seconds in Perth. I was so proud of what I'd achieved, with Harry's help.

chapter 8

Stick up for yourself

AT THE ROME OLYMPICS IN 1960, THE AUSTRALIAN SWIMMING TEAM WAS UNHAPPY FROM THE OUTSET, AS THE MANAGERS HAD SAID WE WEREN'T ALLOWED TO MARCH IN THE OPENING CEREMONY, BECAUSE WE HAD TO COMPETE IN THE FIRST WEEK. I thought that was a huge mistake. It didn't improve morale at all after the long and difficult trip to Rome, which had included an emergency stopover in the incredible heat of Bahrain after the plane experienced engine trouble.

Australia didn't do nearly as well in the pool as it had done in 1956. The boys won four gold medals in Rome (John Devitt, Murray Rose, John Konrads and David Thiele), but I was the only gold medalwinner among the girls. The difference between the two meets was access to our coaches. Harry Gallagher had paid his own way to Rome, although he couldn't get tickets to the pool to see us train or compete. At one point, the actress Elizabeth Taylor came to watch the Australian team, and I told security Harry was part of her entourage just to get him in! It was not until decades later swimmers had professional coaches on the team.

We all travelled outside of Rome so that we could confer with our coaches – we had confidence in them to get us to the next level of competition. I personally had every faith in Mr Gallagher to get me race-fit, and knew that if I had to swim on Wednesday, Coach would have the right training program for each preceding day to get me to the right level.

I shared a room with Lorraine Crapp and Ruth Everuss in Rome. Lorraine had secretly married Dr Bill Thurlow the day before we left Australia and was paranoid that the ASU would find out and fire her. Bill was a medical officer attached to the team, a good 10 years older than Lorraine, which was a real 'no no' as far as her family and the ASU were concerned. She begged us to help keep her secret.

Ruthy and I did our best to cover for her. We had to hide her bed from the manageress and make sure it looked slept in, because she was never there, and when the manageress asked after her we said she was training. We told all the little fibs in the world so Lorraine could spend time with her new husband. We later encouraged her to tell the officials, but she was poorly treated by them, and her training suffered with the distraction. She didn't swim well and retired soon after the Games.

In Rome, we were given one tracksuit each. The rule was that you weren't allowed to walk around the pool with just your swimsuit on, but had to put on your tracksuit as soon as you got out of the water. I had to swim the semi-final and final in one day – the semi in the afternoon and the final at night – and when I was packing my bag to return to the pool for the evening, I found that my tracksuit was still wet. My sister Joyce worked for Larco, who had given me this beautiful, soft, white nylon tracksuit. I'd brought it to wear around the village, but as it was the only one I had dry, I put it in my bag to take to the pool. It had a map of Australia embroidered on it, though not the official Olympic team logo. When I won the gold medal that night, I put the tracksuit on and got up on the dais.

I was quickly reported by the ASU for wearing an unofficial tracksuit. It was painted as, 'Here's Dawn, thumbing her nose at officialdom again', but it was a far more practical issue as far as I was concerned – I didn't want to sit around in a wet tracksuit, as the coaches always told us to stay warm before we swam. Nowadays, of course, they give the swimmers dressing gowns to wear and the athletes have half a dozen tracksuits to choose from.

After I won gold in the 100m, I was competing in the 4 x 100m relay team. The way the team was put together that year was an indication of how poorly we were managed in Rome. They had me swimming first, when they should have had me last, and they had Lorraine down last even though she wasn't training – though we couldn't tell our team manager that this was because we were hiding her secret marriage! Lorraine was always a good starter; even if she ran out of condition in the last five or ten yards, young Ilsa Konrads and Alva Colquhuon could have picked it up, and I might have been able to finish the race off. But it wasn't to be, and the Americans beat us. We took second place.

Back in 1960, I won the national championships in butterfly, setting a world record, so I was chosen to swim the race in the Olympic Games. During training in Townsville, however, I tore muscles on either side of my rib cage and the doctor advised me not to do any more butterfly. I went to the team manager and told him what the doctor had advised – I could still swim freestyle, but if I had to forego one stroke, it had to be butterfly. I then went to the Swimming Association in Townsville and gave them the doctor's certificate. Jan Andrew was nominated to swim in my place.

When we got to Rome, my name was included in the butterfly event. 'I'm not swimming butterfly,' I told the team manager. 'You've seen the doctor's report.'

He said my injury should have healed by now. 'You'll do what you're told,' he said.

'I won't do what I'm told,' I replied. 'I'll do what the doctor has advised, and he has advised me not to swim butterfly. I'm not going to tear those muscles in my stomach again.' He didn't want to hear it. I was 22 – old enough to know my own body – but he was treating me like a 16-year-old.

I contacted Harry Gallagher and told him they wanted me to swim the butterfly leg of the medley. He asked if I was up for it, but I wasn't confident at all. I said I would do the freestyle, then see how I felt and do the butterfly if I could. I won the 100m freestyle but my muscles were suffering afterwards and I decided I couldn't risk another injury.

I had three days off before my next event, during which I got leave to do some sightseeing with my friend Keith Whitehead, and Lorraine Crapp and her new husband. I loved Rome and all its amazing history. We also went to the movies – *Ben Hur* was the big film at the time, and had been shot in Rome the previous year. After my leave, I got back to the village about 3pm and discovered that Bill Slade had been looking for me everywhere. He found me in the dining room. 'Fraser, you've got to swim in an hour,' he said.

'No, I don't,' I told him. 'I'm not swimming until Thursday.' I was set to compete in the heats of the 400m.

'Jan Andrews has made the final in the butterfly, so you have to go and swim the butterfly leg of the relay.'

'Mr Slade, I told you I'm not swimming butterfly against doctor's orders, and besides that, I've just finished dinner. I'd be no good, I'd be more of a hindrance than a help.'

'Jan can't swim because she's swimming the final tomorrow night,' he insisted.

I stuck to my guns – Jan Andrew didn't have to pull out and could swim in the heats. Bill Slade told me he was going to write in the manager's report that I had refused to swim. They didn't include the doctor's certificate in the report and I was eventually stood down for 12 months.

In the end, Alva Colquhuon swam the butterfly leg of the medley, but when Jan finished third in the 100m final, I was accused of costing her the silver. The girls were not happy with me when I pulled out either. Jan and I had a row about it and

I threw a pillow at her, which was petty of me, but it was later exaggerated that I had slapped her. The medley relay qualified for the final in the slowest time, but with Jan and I back in the final, we finished with the silver. I escaped the sometimes bitchy atmosphere by hanging around the boys, who were a bit more carefree and fun, and by watching the men's water polo.

At the end of the Olympics we travelled to Naples for the FINA carnival. We went down by train and they bought a bottle of Chianti for my 22nd birthday coming back. The FINA swim meet didn't go so well. For some reason, I thought I was racing in the 100m, so when I thought the race was done I stopped and stood up – but it was actually a 200m swim, and I was still in the middle of it! Everyone sang out to keep going. Bill Berge Phillips was the vice-president of FINA at the time and he wasn't impressed, but it was a genuine mistake.

We were in Naples for a couple of other reasons, too. Jon Henricks, who'd had a disappointing Olympics after coming down with a case of 'Roman belly', was marrying Bonnie Wilkie there, the sister of US swimmer Mike Wilkie, and many members of the Australian and American swimming squads had been invited. On top of this, I met up with the Neapolitan cousins of our neighbours back home in Balmain, an Italian couple who had always been beautiful to my Mum and Dad – the wife used to call out over the back fence, 'Mrs Rosa, Mrs Rosa, here for you and Papa, a big bowl of spaghetti bolognese.' That's the sort of thing your neighbours did in those days. Their cousins in Naples took me to their house for lunch. They lived on an olive farm, which was absolutely beautiful, and also showed me how they made their own wines.

After this time in Italy, I went to Scotland to visit relatives for a few days, and met up with Harry and his wife Jill in Switzerland on the way. When some school kids came down to watch me swim there, I was accused by the ASU of conducting an 'unauthorised exhibition'. I really couldn't take a trick.

Harry encouraged me to write an apology to the ASU. I did what he suggested, but the apology was rejected and I was left out of successive Australian squads in 1961, sitting on the sidelines of competition for 12 months. I told Harry that I'd had enough of the politics and was going to quit swimming.

That was one of the biggest arguments I ever had with my coach. 'You never supported me,' I cried, 'and you didn't stick up for me in Rome.'

He couldn't, he said, because he wasn't part of the team there. I knew that, of course, but I didn't want to hear it. I wanted to blame someone and I wanted to blame him.

chapter 9

Know that loss is survivable

MY GRANDSON JACKSON IS STARTING TO ASK A LOT OF QUESTIONS. He goes to a local Christian College and enjoys Friday chapel, but recently broke down and said he didn't like God anymore. When I asked why, he said because God took away Conrad, his German Shepherd, and that he's going to hate God when he takes Grandma and his Mum to heaven.

I've been trying to find a way of talking to him about this, because it's obviously playing on his mind. Only the other morning, I saw an opportunity. He came into my room and asked if I was asleep. I had just got back from overseas and was so tired, but when he came in and gave me a kiss, I woke up. Then I started thinking, *What if he wasn't able to wake me up?*

I asked Jackson if I could have a serious talk with him. I asked him what he would do if he couldn't wake me. He said he would go and get Mum, do CPR on me and press down on my chest, ring for an ambulance or go across the road to the neighbours if Mum wasn't with us for any reason. I told him how much it pleased me that he would have the presence of mind to do all of those things if something happened to me.

'But I don't want you to go,' he said.

I told him there was going to be a day when I, too, would be a star in God's heaven, just like Great-grandma and Great-grandpa Fraser, and Great-uncle Donnie, who he never got to meet, and Aunty Rose and Aunty Joyce, and yes, even Conrad. I told him that when we went to Alice Springs later that year, we'd be able to sit under the night sky and see all their stars shining in heaven. And I told him it must be bloody good up there, because nobody comes back to tell us it isn't.

At this stage of his life, that's how I want him to see life. Everything comes to its natural end – people, plants and animals – but we shine on because we have a soul. He's wrestling with some tough questions, but then, we all are.

I lost both my brother and my mother too young, in tragic circumstances, so I understand the grief and sadness that comes with the loss of loved ones. I think back over the past 60 years since Donnie died and there is still pain there, in that he missed out on so much, but I firmly believe he is still with me – inside me – and he continues to be an inspiration to me.

My father suffered from asthma all his life and was a heavy smoker. He had been in ill health for the last decade of his life, and when he passed away on Boxing Day 1961, it was a merciful release, but that did not make it easier for us to take. His death also came at the end of the worst year of my swimming career, when I was suspended for 12 months after the Rome Olympics. I spent Christmas Day with Pop and the family before he passed away, at the age of 75 – the same age I am now. Although I was at a personal and professional low, he encouraged me to keep swimming. My father and I shared a close bond, perhaps because he saw his own sporting dreams realised in me. He had been a good soccer player in his day.

A few years later, in March 1964, I was catching up with family and friends in Sydney after the Nationals. I'd swum a world record 58.9 seconds for the 110 yards, and the 440 yards freestyle in Olympic record time. I was back on track for my third Olympics that year, and better still, Mum had agreed to come to Tokyo to watch me swim for Australia. Sporting organisations in Balmain had banded together to fundraise for her trip and she was very excited about going overseas for the first time, and hopefully seeing me make history.

It was a very busy weekend in Sydney. We had a reunion of sorts at Chequers nightclub on the Friday night and I went to a party at my brother Ken's place on the Saturday night. I spent all day Sunday on the harbour, watching the skiff races, before meeting up with family and friends at Balmain Leagues Club.

At about 10.30pm, Mum asked if I would take my sister Rose home to Kyeemagh, south of Sydney Airport, because she couldn't get a taxi. It had been a long weekend of celebrations and get-togethers, so I'd made the decision not to drink and was OK to drive Rose home. My mother and a friend named

Wendy Walters sat in the back of the car, while Rose was in the front. I was driving a large Pontiac that weekend, a loaner from our family friend Johnny Leitch.

We were travelling along General Holmes Drive towards the airport in a big, heavy car, the first I had ever driven with power steering. As we came around a bend, I noticed a dark shape in the lane closest to the kerb. My friend Wendy yelled at me to watch out and I hit the brakes, but it was too late. The shape was the back end of a pig truck and it ripped into the back of my car, flipping the vehicle over and killing my mother.

I remember being loaded into the ambulance with Wendy, who was badly cut, and asking about my mother and sister. I must have passed out then, because the next thing I remember I was in St George District Hospital. There, I heard someone say, 'Three injured and one DOA', and I knew in my heart Mum was gone. A doctor confirmed this to me before I was sedated.

It was a miracle all of us weren't killed that night. The pig truck had been parked on the side of the road while the owner went off to do a spot of night fishing at Cook's River. I didn't see the truck because it didn't have its lights on, was covered in mud, and was parked in a bad position. The Sydney Coroner, J. J. Loomes, recorded a finding of accidental death during the inquest. He also added a written statement: 'May I through you extend to [Miss Fraser] the sympathy of all associated with this court in this tragic accident – so tragic when the victim is one's own mother. Your client has earned respect and admiration for her deeds as an Olympic representative of the Commonwealth of Australia and I am sure she will find comfort and solace in the thought that she has the sincerest sympathies of a host of people throughout the Commonwealth she has so worthily represented.'

My sister Rosie and my friend Wendy recovered from their injuries, although Wendy's family blamed me for what happened and never spoke to me again. I blamed myself, too, and sank into a deep depression. I had broken several vertebrae in my neck and had to wear a steel brace for nine weeks to immobilise my spine and give it a chance to heal. I was supposed to swim at Tokyo in seven months time, but that was the furthest thing from my mind.

For many years I believed my mother died of a heart attack during the accident, but that was just what my oldest brother Ken told me, to help me cope with the tragedy. He did a lot to help me return to normality, even making me drive his car home when he picked me up from the hospital. It was only his lie about Mum that got me back into a car – I would never have driven again otherwise – and helped me regain my health. It was when I read the official coroner's report in researching documents for my 2001 biography that I discovered the truth. Mum had died, almost instantly, when the car struck the back of the truck and rolled over. Strangely, I had always remembered it to be raining that night, but the coroner's report said it was clear.

Talking about this with my family, and hearing their explanations of why they didn't tell me the truth, helped me come to terms with the accident. They were apologetic, but I understood why they tried to cushion the pain for me. They were trying to help me through a tough time and stop me from blaming myself and going through more hurt. In fact I did experience that hurt later on, when I found out the truth, but I had to be big enough to accept the fact that they did it out of love for me. None of my family blamed me.

Over the years, I've realised you can beat yourself up at night, lose sleep, go over an event in your mind a million times – but you can't change the past. My parents taught me to accept things the way they were, the rights and the wrongs, and to learn from my mistakes. In the same way, I slowly learned to accept what had happened and live with it.

Looking back on that difficult time, I was lucky to have so many friends supporting me in my recovery. I received 500 letters of sympathy and more than 2,000 cards from all kinds of people, including politicians in Australia and rival swimmers from around the world – though not a single word from the ASU. Sir Leslie Herron, the Chief Justice of NSW and the President of the NSW Swimming Association, kindly invited me to morning tea, then asked me to open the Royal Easter Show. I will never forget the warm applause I received when I officially opened the Show, neck brace and all. The Bartlett family in Townsville boarded me during my training for the Tokyo Olympics and they were very, very good to me. Their happy children helped me cope with the pain of Mum's death.

Mum couldn't be there with me in Tokyo, but she was there in my heart. We gave the money that had been raised for her trip to a local charity.

I have been without my mum and dad for almost 50 years now and I still think about them daily. They taught me so much and they loved me unconditionally. That is an incredibly precious thing. I believe it's our duty to move on after suffering loss, and live life to the fullest, but it's also our duty never to forget.

I am the youngest child in my family. My sisters Rose and Joyce passed away within a week of each other. My remaining siblings – Ken, John, Alick and Heather – are elderly, and dealing with health setbacks, but we all retain a positive attitude. Our father always told us to enjoy life, because you're a long time dead, and I'm trying to instill that philosophy in my grandson so that he'll have lots of good memories of us being together.

Embrace every day; that's what I've learned.

chapter 10

Value your teachers

I TRAINED WITH MY COACH HARRY GALLAGHER FOR 15 YEARS – MY ENTIRE SWIMMING CAREER. He was not only my coach, but my mentor and my teacher, too. He was widely respected in the swimming fraternity and no rival ever tried to poach me from him, because everyone knew the special relationship we had. Harry coached the 'whole' person, not just me as a swimmer, and opened my eyes to the wider world. I always tell young swimmers to make sure they find the right coach – not just someone who can train them, but someone they can sit down and talk to, and someone they trust.

For me, Harry was that person. But the ASU never fully utlised Harry's skills.

At the 1964 Tokyo Olympics, I became the first swimmer in history to win a gold medal in the same event in three successive games. For my efforts, I was the given the honour of carrying the Australian flag at the closing ceremony – a task I fulfilled with my ankle heavily strapped – and came home to a hero's welcome. I was named Australian of the Year, and in the New Year I got married.

But I came home from my honeymoon to the news that the ASU had banned me from swimming competitively for ten years. That was effectively a life sentence for a swimmer my age. There was no course for appeal; the decision was made. My swimming career was over.

I had fought so hard to make the Tokyo Olympics and overcome so much. I turned 27 that year, but the ASU still treated me and other members of the squad like children. It was seven weeks of hard work before we headed off overseas, made harder by the fact that I was recovering from a broken neck and still coming to terms with Mum's death. I was the oldest member of the squad and the only one with Olympic experience – the younger girls in the team referred to me as 'Granny'! – but the ASU kept us all on a strict 8.30pm curfew. There was to be no socialising, even when the boys joined us from Ayr, and the communication in camp was very poor. They worked the young girls in the squad far too hard and the overall results in Tokyo were disappointing.

I didn't have good relationships with the people managing the Tokyo preparations. Bill Slade was the manager of the swimming team, and we did not hit it off from the outset, because he was part of the 'old men's club' that ran Australian Swimming and was close to Bill Berge Phillips, the president of the ASU, with whom I'd clashed in the past. I also didn't have my coach, Harry Gallagher, in the immediate lead-up to the Games; he didn't come up to Townsville for training because the ASU has nominated two other coaches, John Bennett and Terry Gathercole, who knew nothing about freestyle swimming. Terry was a breaststroker, only a year older than me. I knew more about what I had to do than Terry ever could, so there was animosity between us there.

Harry had not applied for the Australian coaching job because he was running a pool business in Melbourne and couldn't afford the time away. Nor could he finance a stay in Tokyo during the games. I asked Harry if could send me a swimming schedule because I wasn't happy with the way I was progressing and it was taking a lot of time for me to get back on form in the pool. Having just overcome a serious neck injury, I was struggling with my dive, too. I trained three times a day, at 9am, 1pm and 4pm, and kept nearly entirely to myself.

I had some big arguments with the official coaches about what I was doing and who was actually coaching me. 'Stumpy' Lawrence, the father of swimming coach Laurie Lawrence, used to look after my massaging and help me train, and he was like a father figure to me. He would let me have a lane and was able to time me and keep track of what I was doing. Stumpy also took me over to a little place he had on Magnetic Island on several occasions. 'You're going over there for the weekend,' he told me, 'and you're going to stay there and think about what you're doing in training.' I'd come back on Monday and train like nobody's business.

Before we arrived in Tokyo, we were told that the swimmers would not be permitted to march in the opening ceremony, because we needed the first three days of the Games to prepare for our races. I think this was a huge blow to our stocks in Rome. When you go to an Olympic Games, and you march out in that uniform with the national crest on it, it is the proudest moment. I still get goosebumps today when I recall marching into the MCG at the 1956 Olympics.

In Tokyo, swimming didn't begin until 30 hours after the opening ceremony finished, and my race was 38 hours after that. I could understand the ban if you were swimming within 24 hours, but three days? If I wasn't fit enough to walk around the stadium on opening night and then swim two days later, I shouldn't have been competing! It was a ridiculous decision.

I didn't say anything to the rest of the team, but made the decision to march in the opening ceremony myself. In the end, there were four of us who chose to disobey the ban – Linda McGill, Nan Duncan and Marlene Dayman were the others– although I think only Marlene and I actually marched. I told our manageress, Anne Hatton, that I was going to march because I wasn't swimming for another 38 hours and she said, 'I'll take you to town to get you some white gloves.' She didn't warn me of any repercussions, but I knew Bill Slade would be unhappy with the decision and that it would go into his report.

When we got back from glove shopping, I had my uniform pressed, and when it came time to call the Australian team to the Stadium, I hopped on the bus and sat next to some male athletes, pulling my hat down over my eyes. Bill Slade stood at the bus door and asked if there was anyone on the bus who should not be there. The entire bus said, 'No.' He appeared to be looking straight at me, but he didn't say anything.

When the driver closed the door and we set off, the entire bus yelled, 'Yeah Fras! You made it!'

When we were originally kitted out with our gear for Tokyo, I had sent my swimsuit back to Speedo be fixed. It was one-and-a-half inches too short, so the five judges would have got an eyeful when I bent over, and I was so unhappy with it that I had to send it back three times. Finally I decided to make my own swimsuit because I'd had so much trouble finding an official suit to fit my frame. I'm a dressmaker by trade, so I got some material and made a swimsuit that would fit my body. I gave my prototype to a rival swimwear company and they gave me a couple of costumes in my size, which I packed.

I wore my homemade swimsuit in the heats and semi-finals of the 100m, after which the team's Chef de Mission called me in and asked me to explain myself. I showed him both swimsuits – the one I was given and the one that I wore – and asked if he could see the difference. Then I put on the official swimsuit, stood up on his desk, and bent over. 'See what I mean,' I said. I showed him the difference in my homemade suit. Who knows what he thought of these demonstrations!

'Why didn't you say something?' he asked me. I told him I had, three times! Nevertheless, I was instructed to wear the official swimsuit in the final, no matter what the potential embarrassment might be.

On the day of the final, I had a bad asthma attack, and the

team doctor, Howard Toyne, said I might have to pull out. From my perspective, that was never going to happen. He gave me some tablets and I used my asthma spray before I went to the pool, but I'm sure all the stress over the swimsuit didn't help. Nor did the official costume, which was so tight across my broad chest that it actually constricted my breathing.

I made a few mistakes in the race. I went out too slow in the first 50m and the American Sharon Stouder pressed me all the way to the finish line on the second lap. Fortunately, I still won the gold with a yard to spare, breaking the minute (59.5) to set a new Olympic record, but missing out on breaking my existing world record (59.2). I was the first Australian to win a gold medal at those Olympics and had the honour of seeing the national flag raised for the first time in Tokyo.

After the highs of Melbourne eight years before, Australian swimming had rested on its laurels for a long time, and that was reflected in our gold medal tally in Tokyo, halved from eight to four since Melbourne. My coach Harry Gallagher was a world away and it was hard not to have him there at the proudest moment of my career. I was the only individual female to medal, although the 4 x 100m medley relay finished a fair second to the US. The Americans placed Sharon Stouder first, while the managers put me last, and I swam an unofficial world record of 58.6 seconds for the final leg (this was before electronic timing, and because I hadn't started the race, my time was recorded unofficially).

In the heats of the 400m freestyle, Nan Duncan, Kim Herford and I wore the spare 'unofficial' swimsuits that I'd brought, but we were instructed by coach Terry Gathercole to wear the official ones in the final. Kim obeyed this edict, but I didn't. The instruction had come from the very top – Bill Berge Phillips – so I knew there would be trouble at the end of the Games. I finished fifth in the final because I hadn't trained properly for the race, making the 100m my main focus instead. Rumours circulated that I hadn't tried, but of course, that wasn't the case.

The coaches who had helped us be so competitive in Melbourne were sadly missing in Rome and Tokyo and our results suffered accordingly. It was Harry who was able to give me the mental approach to win. When I got close the minute mark in Rome in 1960, it was Harry who put the idea in my head that I could break the minute.

After Tokyo, I even thought, *Well, there's only another four years to Mexico City. Can I do it? Can I improve even further?* I trusted Harry as a coach, and I knew my own ability when I set my mind to something.

Back when I was first living in Adelaide, I had drawn a picture of a stepladder with four steps on it and put it behind my door. Those steps led to the Olympic Games in Melbourne, the Commonwealth Games in Cardiff, the Olympic Games in Rome and the Commonwealth Games in Perth, each step representing a space of two years and a new goal. I had exceeded that ladder already by going to Tokyo in 1964. Having reached the top of the ladder, I wondered if it was the end of my swimming career.

Then, of course, there was the 'flag' business.

chapter 11

If you want something, ask first

WHETHER I AM TALKING TO SCHOOLCHILDREN, OR AT FUNCTIONS WITH PEOPLE MY OWN AGE, I'M ALWAYS ASKED ABOUT THE EPISODE WITH THE OLYMPIC FLAG AT THE END OF THE 1964 TOKYO GAMES. I tell the truth about what happened that day, but I also try to turn the incident into a positive story so that it can inspire people to learn from my mistakes.

The furore that resulted over my decision to indulge in a moment of larrikinism and souvenir an official Olympic flag from the Imperial Palace has in some ways overshadowed my entire career. People still think this was the reason I was banned by the Australian Swimming Union for 10 years, even though the issues were completely separate and had nothing to do with my performance in the pool. I ended up successfully suing the ASU for defamation on this point, and journalist

Ernie Christensen for reporting that this incident was behind the ban.

If I'd known the consequences of taking the flag in 1964, I would have named the other people involved and cleared my name, but I felt I couldn't dob in these two mates, the team doctor and a hockey player, who set out with me that night. The truth is that, yes, I was there, but I wasn't the one who climbed the flagpole; I never could never have climbed it myself.

During the Tokyo Games, film producer Lee Robinson was making a documentary about my career. Robinson and his crew, including scriptwriter Joy Cavill, had filmed me in Townsville and the Olympic Village at Yoyogi, and I was given permission to leave the village a week before the Games ended to continue filming at the Imperial Palace Hotel. We visited many of Tokyo's nightclubs, cabarets and geisha houses, and wherever I went, the Japanese people showed me great respect and kindness because I had won the gold medal. They called me 'Don Fraser-san'.

While I was in Tokyo shooting the documentary, Australian team manager Len Curnow informed me, after a party at the Australian Embassy, that I had been chosen to carry the Australian flag in the closing ceremony. I was a popular selection, he said, and would be the first woman to carry the flag in an Olympic closing ceremony. It was a wonderful honour, and put the fact that Bill Slade had reported me to the ASU to the back of my mind.

The night before the closing ceremony, the Australian men's hockey team had won the bronze medal and came back to the hotel where I was staying in high spirits. We were invited to their party, and because I had finished competing, I had a few drinks and entered into the festivities. In the early hours of the morning, Dr Howard Toyne and hockey player Des Piper suggested we souvenir some Olympic flags in Tokyo – the classic white flag with the Olympic rings – so we left the party to do just that.

Close to the Imperial Place, there were flags on flagpoles, spaced about 50 yards apart. Howard and I held Des up, as he was the lightest, and soon we had two flags. Des was actually throwing the third flag to the ground when we heard the whistles blast.

'Run! Here come the police!'

I picked up the third flag and put it under my tracksuit. Quickly, we separated. I ran up a steep rise towards some bushes, where I hid. It was still quite dark, but I could see the police searching for us. We hid for a while before the boys made a dash for it and I finally felt it was safe to go to. As I jumped over a wall, I twisted my ankle, but I was running on adrenalin – and having great fun in the adventure of it all – when I became entangled in barbed wire on a hedge. Unfortunately, there was a pond on the other side of the hedge, and as I freed myself I fell into it, waist deep.

I stayed there for about 15 minutes before slowly walking out, cold and smelly, with my flag still tucked up inside my tracksuit. I climbed back over the hedge and sat down on a park bench to catch my breath and work out what to do when two police officers came up to me and asked me to come with them. I tried to escape on a bike that was lying beside a police hut on the way out of the park, but was not successful, and was forced to go to Maranouchi Police Station.

I had been selected to carry the Australian flag at the closing ceremony later that day and was scared that I had blown that opportunity. I had no ID on me and when I was asked by an English-speaking officer what my name was, I said, 'Dawn Fraser.'

'No, no, no,' the officer said. 'Don Fraser-san, she not do something like this.'

'Oh yes she would,' I said.

He allowed me to make a phone call and I called Lee Robinson. It was three in the morning and he was less than happy to receive my call. I told him we had been arrested for trying to take Olympic flags and asked him to bring my ID and gold medal to the police station to prove my identity. By this time I was extremely embarrassed. When Superintendent Kamira, the head of the police station, suggested I was a 'very naughty girl' I had to agree with him. I wrote them a letter of apology and signed it, and the police had their photos taken with me. I was not charged with any offence.

Superintendent Kamira said something to me that I will always remember. 'If you want a souvenir,' he said gently, 'you go into a shop and buy a souvenir. You don't pull a flag down from where it is flying, especially near the Imperial Palace. That is stealing and that is a jail sentence in our country.'

I was very sorry indeed, and more than happy to sign a letter of apology for what I had done, also promising that I would never, ever do it again. I was afraid the incident would be leaked to the papers and affect the final day at the Olympics, but the Japanese police were really wonderful about it all.

My ankle was quite sore, so after Lee arrived and confirmed my identity, they carried me downstairs. I suggested they keep my gold medal and give me the flag, but the police refused the offer. Superintendent Kamira put the gold medal around my neck and sent me on my way.

Howard and Des were not carrying the flags they had grabbed when they were arrested, so they were not charged with any crime either, and for the next three decades their involvement in the escapade remained a secret. I was disappointed that neither of them spoke up when the matter played out in the press after my disqualification, but I certainly wasn't going to name them. Des Piper later broke his silence after he was named manager of the Olympic hockey team.

I had my ankle wrapped by a doctor at the Imperial Palace Hotel so that I'd be able to walk in the closing ceremony. After I left for the village, Superintendent Kamira came to the hotel carrying a large box, and gave it to Lee Robinson. It was the Olympic flag, along with a note: 'With compliments from the police.' It was a wonderful gesture on his part. I called into the police station before I left with a little gift for him – a gold kangaroo pin – but he wasn't there. It was another decade before we met again.

When I got back to the village that Saturday morning, the first person I went to was Len Curnow. I told him the story, saying, 'Look, this morning at about half past one, a couple of us went out and souvenired some Olympic flags. We got caught by the police, but they let us off, and I wrote a note apologising to the Emperor. The other two people were arrested, but I didn't get locked up, because they couldn't believe it was me. They even gave me the bloody flag,' I finished incredulously.

I asked Len if he was going to put the incident in his report, and Len said it has nothing to do with the Olympic team. 'Don't worry, it will be all right,' he said.

It wouldn't be in his report – but it was in Bill Slade's.

With my ankle heavily strapped, I carried the Australian flag in the closing ceremony; nothing was going to stop me from marching at the front of the team. I swapped hats with Bill Northam, the yachting great, and wore his hat instead of my deerstalker. I actually did the ankle more damage by marching, and by the time I arrived back in Australia, I had to use a wheelchair to get off the plane. When people asked how I injured my ankle, I just said, 'Too much dancing.'

Unfortunately I was due to take part in a FINA carnival at Osaka after the Olympics. I had not been keen to take part in the carnival anyway, after the problems I'd had in Naples in 1960, but my injury ruled me out for sure. That might have been the straw that broke the camel's back as far as Bill Berge Phillips was concerned. His response to my 'troubles in Tokyo' would send us both to the law courts.

Life is not about regrets, it's about learning. You make mistakes and you learn from them. And I did. I shouldn't have stolen the flag – I should have asked for it. I was talked into doing something stupid, and many before me have done the same – you'd be surprised the number of letters I've received from athletes who say they still have the flags they stole! And in fact, I still have that Olympic flag myself. It holds pride of place among the treasures of my career.

In the late 1970s I was the subject of a *This is Your Life* program hosted by Roger Climpson (I was also featured in a *This is Your Life* episode in 2001, hosted by Mike Munro … that's two lifetimes!). Imagine my surprise when Climpson introduced Superintendent Kamira as a special guest.

chapter 12

Treasure the support of your family

GARY WARE WAS AN EXTROVERT. He was good-looking and he smoked cigarettes and he seemed to have a lot to do with racehorses – backing them, owning them, and spending money on them.

Horses were my first love, so I thought we had a lot in common, but Gary was a bookmaker and a professional punter, which proved to be a volatile mix. Although he was possessive and sometimes domineering, I fell in love with him. That turned out to be a mistake. I was planning for the long term, while Gary was living day to day.

Why didn't I see it coming? Well, I guess sometimes you don't want to see it. Everyone goes into a relationship wanting it to work, but sometimes the person you marry is not who you think they are.

I first met Gary in Townsville in 1964, when I was training for the Tokyo Olympics, and the last thing I wanted was to fall in love. After a Saturday of training, Linda McGill, Jan Turner and I headed into town for a well-deserved night out, although we weren't drinking. Gary was at the Allen Hotel with a group of jockeys and we hit it off. We chatted and had a couple of dances and he invited me out the next day to a game of rugby league. He didn't show, and I should have taken that as an omen, but we started going out.

When Gary came around where I was boarding with the Bartlett family, they warned me that he had 'a name' in town, and to be very careful. They were like my parents, even though they were only a few years older than me, but I didn't listen.

When we started getting serious, I said to Gary, 'I'm up here for training and I need to spend a lot of time training.' I found it hard to get in the pool when I had a relationship on my mind, and I even broke it off for a while so I could concentrate on training for Tokyo, but that didn't last long.

We talked about getting married and about what I wanted to do in the future. I knew that I didn't want to have a baby straight away, as I didn't think I was finished with swimming yet. I wanted to go on for another two years and qualify for the 1966 Commonwealth Games in the West Indies. We ended up getting engaged before I left for Tokyo in September 1964, and planned to marry in January 1965. The way my mother raised the girls in our family, it was important that we waited until we were married before we had sex, and basically we couldn't wait any longer.

He saw me off at the airport when I left for Tokyo and I think he was shocked by the media attention. He seemed very uncomfortable about it, but I assured him that soon, all that would be in the background, and I would be Mrs Gary Ware. After I left for Tokyo, Gary went to Sydney to meet my family. He stayed at our house in Balmain, where my brother Alick was still living.

When I returned to Australia, having won the fourth gold medal of my career but once again fallen foul of the ASU, we were invited to the Melbourne Cup as guests of honour. We were paraded down the Flemington straight in front of 85,000 people in an open car – a gesture usually reserved for members of the royal family – and I think Gary even backed the Cup winner, Polo Prince. A tragic, hectic, controversial and ultimately successful 1964 was capped when I was named Australian of the Year.

We were married in Sydney, as planned, on 30 January 1965. I had saved up a bit of money and ended up paying for everything, although we had the use of the cars for nothing and the reception was held at the Town Hall. My girlfriend from Melbourne came up to be my maid of honour and organised my nephew's fiancée to be my bridesmaid. It was a lovely wedding, but our marriage was doomed from the very start – I found out later that Gary was having an affair with the singer we had brought down from Townsville for the reception.

Gary and I went on our honeymoon in Vanuatu, but on the day we got back, there were newspaper headlines up and down Pitt Street: 'Dawn Banned 10 Years.'

'What did you get up to in Tokyo?' Gary asked.

'Nothing to get ten years for,' I told him.

When I contacted my brother Alick, he said, 'Sis, there's a letter here for you.' I got the letter from him; it was the official complaint from the ASU. It said I had to give a good reason why I shouldn't be banned for ten years after I had marched in the opening ceremony and not worn the regulation swimsuit in the semi-final – there was nothing in the letter about my escapades with the Olympic flag. The date for answering the complaint in person had passed while I was on my honeymoon.

I rang my solicitor Ted France and said, 'I think you need to see this.' I took the letter and showed it to him.

'Ten years for this?' he said.

I successfully sued the ASU and sports journalist Ernie Christensen from *The Sun*, who reported that there had been 'bigger issues' behind my disqualification, including the Olympic flag episode. But the court action took more than three years and in that time I wasn't allowed to train with any other person. That was very difficult. I could have done it, but I was so disgusted with the way the Australian Swimming Union had treated me, I thought, *Do I really need this?* I was married, so I decided I would have a baby.

But there were already problems with my marriage. Gary's love of gambling caused conflicts between us. He owned a couple of good horses – Booberanna was a stayer, while Song of Mine was a sprinter, and Booberanna had won the Townsville Cup in July 1964. Gary had given me a share in the horse as an engagement present.

I can still remember the day we won the New Year's Gift with Booberanna. I received the check for £25,000 pounds and the trainer Jim Griffiths said, 'Dawn, make sure you put this in the bank.' I took my hat off and put it under there so I wouldn't lose it. No sooner had I hopped off the winner's dais, though, than Gary wanted the cheque. I asked him why, and he said he had to pay it out to bookmakers, as he had lost the money on other races. I knew then and there that we would never have the financial security we needed.

Gary wanted me to live in Townsville and I agreed for a while, but I was heavily pregnant and missed my family. Just before our daughter was born in December 1965 – we named her Dawn-Lorraine, in honour of Lorraine Crapp – we returned to Sydney to live in the family home. My parents had loved living there and it was always my dream to buy it. I had a little money saved from my swimming days, so I went to see Ted France again. 'Put the home in your name – Dawn Fraser,' he told me.

'But I'm Mrs Gary Ware,' I replied.

I think he could see what was happening, even if I couldn't. 'If you get divorced, you'll go back to your own name,' he said.

'Ted, I'm not going to get divorced!'

'Well, then, it won't matter.'

Two years later, I was a single mother. If I hadn't put the house in my name, I would have lost everything – everything.

Moving to Sydney was the worst thing that could have happened to Gary. He gambled and drank, and although he stayed out womanising, he was becoming increasingly jealous of my long-standing friendships. I had introduced him to people who gave him credit to gamble, but he did so against my good name – these were people who would break your legs if they couldn't collect. I knew Lenny McPherson, a colourful underworld figure at the time, and got along well with him, so I phoned him and said, 'I'm sorry I introduced my husband to you, I didn't realise he was like this.' Lenny said it wasn't my problem and that he'd look after it.

But when Gary came home drunk after losing money, and bashed me over the head when I was in bed, especially with a little baby, I drew the line. I had never been hit by a man in my life, and when the physical abuse started, it was horrible. I used to be frightened of him coming home drunk; I could fight my battles verbally, but I never could have hit anyone.

Eventually, there was an occasion when he was coming up the stairs drunk, shouting abuse at me, asking where I had been and I snapped. I broke the baby's glass bottle on the step and said, 'If you come any closer I'll jab this in you, so please go downstairs and get out of the house. I don't want to go to jail for you.'

Gary left. I called my brother and asked him to come round, then locked the door and put chairs up against it. Alick had got on well with Gary, but blood was thicker than water. When Gary turned up the next day and tried to come in, I threw him down a bag packed with his belongings, and said, 'Don't you ever come back.' As much as it broke my heart to end the marriage, I didn't know what Gary was capable of, especially when drunk, and I had a child to protect.

Gary returned to Townsville and had only sporadic contact with Dawn-Lorraine in the ensuing years. It was another big hurt for me – the loss of a relationship, of a future together, and the possibility of financial security that comes with that. The end of my marriage shook the foundations of everything that I'd been taught about family and I wondered how I could ever trust anyone again. On top of that, I was a single mum with a baby daughter, but I wasn't scared of that – I had the support of my family and I had always been a hard-working woman.

My family home in Balmain, which I still own, has been a great asset over the years and has allowed me to invest in my future, and my daughter and grandson's future. I later rang my solicitor and thanked him for his advice.

'What did I do?' he asked.

'You sly old fox,' I said. 'You made me put the house in my name because you knew.'

Gary and I were officially divorced in 1968 and I never married again. I would have loved to be married, and maybe had three or four children, but it just didn't happen and I'm content with how things have turned out. I was a champion swimmer. That was the path I chose, and in many ways, it was the path that chose me. Today, I've got lovely relationships with all the members of my family.

***

The day I got the sack from *Celebrity Apprentice*, I spent two hours with a young woman from Chris Riley's Youth off the

Streets program, which very much affected me. When I sat down with her, she just took my hand and said she felt very comfortable with me. 'Well, what do you want to talk about, darling?' I asked. Then I just sat back and listened as she told me the story of her life.

She had been abused by her father from the age of five, abused by her two brothers, and continuously raped throughout her childhood. She started using drugs when she was 12, was a single mother at 18, and was still on drugs. 'Dawn, I have a three-month-old baby and I'm working now,' she said. 'I take the child to work with me. I'm off drugs and I don't smoke and I don't drink alcohol. My child is my number one priority.'

'Does it get to you?' I asked.

'Sometimes,' she said, 'and it's very hard, but not as hard as the life I used to have.'

That was just the best answer I could imagine. I had so much respect for this young girl, and I wished she was my daughter, so I could have helped her and prevented her from experiencing all that pain

We sat in the garden for two hours. Before I left, I gave her my phone number and told her if there was anything I could ever do to help, she should ring me. She called the next day and thanked me for listening to her story.

This young woman moved me so much, I could hardly speak about it. I don't usually show my emotions, but when I had to talk about it that night on television, I was in tears. The thing was, speaking to her about her life, I saw how incredibly lucky I am. I've always had family support to help me through the tough times. If you don't have that in your life, you need to find it, from anywhere you can – like this young woman saw fit to trust in me.

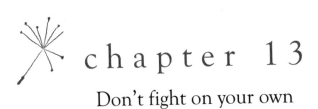

chapter 13

Don't fight on your own

By May 1966, my marriage was over, I was still suing the ASU and *The Sun*, and my dream of representing Australia at a record fourth Olympics in Mexico was slipping away. The court case against Bill Berge Phillips was bogged down in legal argument until his secretary came forward and gave my legal team copies of five letters he had dictated to her to send out to swimming officials around the world. 'It is a pity that the world greatest swimmer should be a person such as this,' Berge Phillips had written.

He eventually made a public apology and the matter was settled out of court, but he refused to shake my hand, and the written apology he was instructed to forward to me never eventuated. The terms of the settlement were confidential, but at least I could apply to have my ten-year ban lifted.

It was a hollow victory. The ban was lifted within eight weeks of the court decision, in March 1968, but I had missed the Nationals in February and did not have enough time to prepare for the Olympics. More than that, I had a baby to look after, and I didn't want to put her, the love and joy of my life, second. So I drew the line and announced my retirement at the age of 31. Nowadays, female athletes are able to leave their sport to have a baby, then have the financial security to continue their career afterwards, as Evonne Goolagong Cawley did when she came back and won Wimbledon in 1980. But that wasn't possible in the sixties.

In 1968, the Olympic organising committee invited me to the Mexico Games. Harry Gallagher was over there as a coach, so I accepted the invitation. There was part of me that didn't want to let go of my swimming career and I still wanted to be a part of the Olympic family. I did a bit of training before I went – I guess I wanted to show the 'big boys' that I still had it – then headed off to Mexico, leaving Dawn-Lorraine in the care of my sister Joyce.

During the Games, Judy-Joy Davis, a former Olympian who was working as a newspaper reporter, bet me $100 that I couldn't break 62 seconds for the 100m. With Harry acting as the time-keeper, I swam 60.2 seconds – good enough to win the bet and good enough, it turned out, to have won a silver medal at the Mexico Olympics.

I had to come back to Australia before the end of the Olympics to give evidence in the defamation case I'd brought against *The Sun*, but I almost missed the plane home, because

I was determined to watch the final of the 100m women's freestyle. American Jan Henne won it in 60 seconds flat; it was somewhat gratifying to me that she couldn't beat the time I'd set in Tokyo four years before. I was 31 years old and had done only minimal training in the past six months, but I had no doubt in my mind I could have won a gold in Mexico. I had improved my time at every Olympics and I am sure I would have bettered my Tokyo time under Harry's training.

In October 1968 I was awarded damages against *The Sun* for an article Ernie Christensen wrote about the 'real reason' behind my ten-year ban. We won $10,000, and while Associated Newspapers appealed the ruling, it was upheld in the Supreme Court.

After my marriage to Gary ended, I met rugby league player Graeme Langlands at a Sydney nightspot called the Motor Club. He was there with a few of his mates, Johnny 'Chook' Raper and Billy Smith, and we hit it off straight away. Although he was a couple of years younger than me, and I had a daughter underfoot, Graeme and I started going out and we had a lot of fun together. It was just the sort of relationship I needed at the time and I thought there was a real future for us. It was a different story with 'Changa', Langlands' mother. She did not approve of her son going out with a single mother who was older than him, and not even properly divorced yet.

We went out for about two years and I truly believe we loved each other, but in the middle of 1969, I was contacted by Graeme's mother. I had never spoken to her before, but what she told me was a bombshell – I wasn't to see her son anymore because he was getting married, she told me. He had got another of his girlfriends pregnant and was going to do the right thing and marry her. Graeme and I tried to talk it through, but at the time I wasn't divorced, so I wasn't in any position to make demands of him. It saddened me greatly the way things worked out and I shed a lot of tears over the breakup.

After that, coupled with the realisation that I could have been very competitive in Mexico if I had continued my career, I started to spiral into a depression and fell into a black hole. I had no direction, no idea where I was going in life. After having been so focused for so long, the reality was that my swimming career had been taken away from me. I hadn't been able to leave on my own terms.

I knew I was depressed, because I was struggling so much, and eventually had to ask Joyce to come and care for Dawn-Lorraine for a time. I was very fortunate that I had a family who was looking out for me. I could have ended up anywhere – on drugs, or an alcoholic, or in the gutter somewhere. But because my family were so supportive of me and could see what was happening, they were always in touch and encouraging me: 'Come on, sis, you've got to get yourself out of this.'

I remember going to a party in our street one night, two doors down, like you did in those days. My daughter was only about 18 months old and I took her with me in her basinet. The party-goers included entertainers from Les Girls, who knew me and my brother pretty well. One of the Les Girls gave me a puff of a cigarette. I didn't know it at the time, but it was marijuana, and it made me so violently ill that I immediately knew I had to get home. I called Joyce to come and get the baby, wondering all along how anyone could smoke marijuana if that was how it affected them. For the next twenty four hours, I just lay beside a bucket, and today if I smell marijuana anywhere, I've got to walk!

My family were very good to me during this period in my life. They would constantly make contact with me and ensure I was looking after myself and my daughter, and I always felt I could talk to them about things. Having my daughter also helped, because when you're a parent, you realise you have someone else to look after and it's not all about you. We had neighbours in the local community who cared, and many became like an adopted family to us. I was very friendly with Mum's older friends at the local pub, especially a lady we called 'Red' who told me some home truths about myself at that time – specifically that Mum would not have approved of me dropping my bundle and giving up on myself. Red was like a second mother for me and made sure I was looking after myself.

Many families don't have those 'significant elders' in their lives to guide them through tough times. Rising stars might not want or allow older people to give them advice, but then there comes the inevitable time when their careers are over and they need someone to talk to. I've seen this happen so often with sportspeople. They experience the highs of competition and success, but when it suddenly ends, it is difficult to deal with reality.

I can relate to those athletes who miss the energy and routine of their careers when they retire, and feel there's no pathway for them afterwards. I can also identify with young mums who go through that difficult spiral after having a baby. It wasn't called depression in my day, but we now know much more about the 'black dog' so many people suffer with.

If you are struggling with depression, don't be isolated. Don't try and deal with it by yourself, because you can't. I've been there, and I survived. And so can you.

chapter 14
Seek advice

IN THE MID-1970S, THE LEASE FOR THE RIVERVIEW HOTEL IN BIRCHGROVE CAME UP. It was my family's favourite watering hole. Dad and my brothers used to drink there in the afternoon and meet up with Mum on a Friday night. I remember sitting on the back of a coal truck having a 'juico', then carrying Dad's work bag home from the pub. In those days, the bar would close at six, so patrons would down their drinks in a hurry (the 'six o'clock swill') before walking home for dinner. It's what a lot of working-class families did of an afternoon.

The Riverview was a second home to us. What a lot of people don't realise about pubs in the 1950s and 1960s is that they were often the centre of the local community. I used to go up there after school and run messages for the women sitting in the ladies bar – they used to sit there peeling their vegetables for the evening meal – while they drank a shandy. Mum and all her neighbours would congregate there, and no men were allowed, unless they were accompanying a lady.

When the lease came up, I signed on for five years. I thought it was a good business opportunity and a great way to stay connected with the local community. I was the licensee and I had three partners, two of whom didn't work in the pub, so the other partner and I did virtually everything – restocking the cellar, cleaning the bar and the toilets, replenishing the snack bar … We had a rowdy clientele of locals and football players, so it was pretty full on. The fact that I was serving behind the bar probably encouraged some people to come in and have a drink or two. Sometimes there were so many people that they drank out on the footpath, which we'd get into trouble for with the local police.

It was a pretty tough lifestyle for me, as a single parent. Ten o'clock closing had come in, and then the state government allowed Sunday trading, so we worked seven days a week. I had already made the decision to enroll Dawn-Lorraine in boarding school at St Vincent's College at Potts Point. My good friend Jack Stanistreet helped me get her in, as I wasn't Catholic, and the sister in charge was a beautiful person who understood my situation. I was a single mum, I had a business to run, and I wanted a great education for my daughter, so it was the best thing for her to board at the time, and I still got to see her every weekend.

There are a lot of financial issues in the running of a pub, and it's very hard to make a dollar when there are four of you in the partnership. Two of the partners had their accountant take care of the books, so sometimes cheques were signed unbeknownst to me, with a lot of money going out of the business that I wasn't aware of. There were long hours, sometimes 20 a day, starting at six in the morning until the early hours of the next, and I soon realised it was very different being the licensee than a local drinker enjoying myself with the clientele. And of course, everyone wanted to have a drink with me – the locals, the visitors, busloads of Japanese tourists, friends and celebrities.

One night in 1981, I was due to go to another hotel for a function. We closed at 10pm and normally would wash the floors and open all the louvres in the windows and toilets, as well as the doors to the cellars, to get rid of the smell of stale smoke and beer. I raced around the counter to get 20 cents for the phone, to call the other hotel and let them know I was on my way, but I slipped on the wet floor and slid through the open cellar door, down the steps to the cellar, trying to get a hold of anything on my way, and finally finishing all the way at the bottom of the stairs. I didn't know it at the time, but I re-broke the vertebrae in my neck in that fall and badly damaged my knee. I still made it to the other hotel for the end of the function, but was sick and sore the following morning, when I had to fly to Melbourne for a meeting with the Confederation of Australian Sport.

On the plane, I was in so much pain – I didn't realise I had hurt myself so badly. I told the hostess I'd had a fall the previous night, and she said, 'Don't move.' She wrapped a hand towel around my neck and then gave me a painkiller. In Melbourne, I was staying at the home of Raelene Boyle, the great sprint athlete, and as soon as she saw me she called her doctor. The doctor thought I was having a heart attack, as I was in so much pain and experiencing pins and needles down my arm. After an X-ray, though, he could see the damage. He said he needed to inject dye into my system to determine the full extent of the injuries.

All I wanted to do was get back to my own doctor in Sydney. I stayed with Raelene in Melbourne for a week, lying on the floor, then got myself back to Sydney, loaded up with painkillers and wearing a neck brace. My friend Peggy Carter had her doctor look at me. He called an ambulance and sent me straight to St Vincent's Hospital.

As it turned out, I had three chipped vertebrae, a pinched spinal chord and bone fragments floating in my spinal fluid. I spent two weeks in hospital with my neck packed in sand to support the injury, and it took an operation and two months of slow recovery to get back on my feet. Even then, I still had pain down my side and was partially paralysed – I even had to learn to use a knife and fork again. Dawn-Lorraine, who was attending business college at the time, took up the slack by working behind the scenes, cleaning and restocking, but it was the end of my pub career as I couldn't do the physical work.

When I was a publican, I took up smoking. It was more social than anything else – the cigarette salesmen would come in and offer you his products, and I'd put them out on the bar and have a puff. Most of my girlfriends smoked, as did the customers, and even though my father had died of lung cancer and I was a bad asthmatic, it was a habit I easily slipped into after my swimming career ended.

While I was flat on my back in hospital, I asked Peggy to go and buy me a pack of cigarettes. She really disapproved of smoking, so she just looked at me incredulously. 'You're asking me to go and buy you cigarettes?'

'Please, I'm dying for one,' I said.

She went and got me a packet, opened it up for me, and put the packet on my chest. 'That's the last time you'll ever see me, then,' she said.

'Hey,' I said, 'what are you talking about? They're only cigarettes.'

'You smoke any of those and you'll never see me as a friend again,' she said. Then she left.

I put the cigarettes in a drawer and gave up smoking then and there. There I was, lying in hospital, and asking my friend to bring me cigarettes when it was against her principles. Smoking certainly wasn't worth the loss of her friendship.

When the hospital bills had to be paid, there was no money – the accountant appointed by one of my silent partners had not paid my medical insurance. Fortunately I was able to get through my rehabilitation with the help and support of family and friends, and a fundraiser at the Sydney Entertainment Centre, organised by friends, helped pay my hospital fees. But if the accountant hadn't paid my medical insurance, I figured he probably hadn't paid other bills for the pub too. I had a very good relationship with the brewery, Tooheys, because I was one of the first publicans to put Tooheys New on tap, but when I tried to buy the lease in my own name, they said I was behind in my payments and owed about $85,000. That was a lot of money in the early 1980s (still is today!). I went to see them about my predicament and they gave me the option of 'trading out' – effectively working off the debt over time, as much as I could pay per week. I also reported the accountant to the Chartered Accountants Association in Canberra, but we didn't get any of our money back.

This was the main lesson I took from running a pub for five years – I should have sought independent financial advice. It also taught me how important it is to keep a close eye on the books and pay the bills yourself, rather than giving that authority to other people.

Five years to the day since I bought the place, I walked out of the pub with less money than I had when I started, not to mention in enormous debt, but we finished on a high note when I put on the last couple of kegs for free and invited all the regulars over for a farewell drink. I had never worked harder in my life, and though I had very little to show for it, what a party we had to end it all.

Still recovering from my injuries, I was nearly bankrupt, and mortified that I could lose everything, including my family home. I was on an invalid pension while I recuperated, but when I was strong enough, I secured a coaching job at the Sydney University pool and started paying off my debt. The manager of the United Permanent Building Society was a regular swimmer at the pool, training there after open heart surgery – the big scar down his chest was a giveaway. He was swimming all by himself, splashing about a bit and struggling, and I suggested he let me coach him. After about a month, he actually became quite a good swimmer.

One day, out of the blue, he remarked, 'I hear you're in some financial trouble, Dawn.'

'I am, but I'm working it off,' I said.

'How much do you owe?' he asked me. When I told him I had about $65,000 left to pay, he gave me his business card and said to come and see him at his office in Petersham the next morning.

'Right!' he said, when I showed up at the appointed hour. 'Let's see what we can do for you. Do you own a house?'

'I own my parents' house in Balmain,' I said.

'Do you have a mortgage?'

I didn't.

'How much do you think the house is worth?'

'About $55,000?' I suggested.

'If it's a terrace house in Balmain, it's worth double that,' he told me. 'I can give you a mortgage on the house and you can pay off the debt to the brewery. You can pay your mortgage out at far less interest.'

I had been with the Bank of NSW all my life, but they wouldn't help me with a loan because I was a single mother. So I decided to switch to United Permanent, who were later bought out by the ANZ Bank, and I've been with them ever since. It was wise advice indeed.

I enjoyed working as a swim coach at the Sydney University

pool; I took a squad of swimmers to the University Games in Korea in the 1980s and we won quite a few events. My daughter Dawn-Lorraine joined me at the pool soon after I started and we ran learn-to-swim classes there. We were doing that for almost ten years, until I went into politics in 1988, at which point Dawn-Lorraine took over the school while I worked part-time as an attendant. It was great to see my daughter get involved in coaching; she was very good at it.

After a regime change at Sydney University, a former Olympian came in and paid a large fee to take over the business we had built. When they only stayed for a year, the university asked me to come back, but I felt like I couldn't trust them anymore – what if they sold it out from under us again? I still wanted to coach children, but I had moved on and I didn't want to go back.

The important thing I took away from my financial problems during the early 1980s was not to be afraid to talk to someone. I was embarrassed to get advice, as I knew money just wasn't lent to single women or divorcees in those days. I was a breadwinner, but that didn't make any difference – I was a female. Today, discrimination like that doesn't happen so much anymore.

chapter 15

Don't let a relationship define you

I HAVE BEEN ALONE IN MY LIFE, BUT NEVER LONELY.

My first love was a Catholic boy, a 'surfie' from Bondi named Michael Hall. When I was in Melbourne for the 1956 Olympics, he was there competing in a surf life-saving competition, and we met through friends. When I brought him home to Balmain after the Olympics, though, my father threw a bucket of water over us and told him to go home. 'Dawn's not going to see you anymore,' Pop declared, 'because you're Catholic.' The funny thing was, my mother was a Catholic!

I was angry at my father at the time – I was 18 years old, to all intents and purposes an adult, and already nationally known as an Olympian – but I knew Dad had my best interests at heart. Michael and I have laughed about it when we caught up over the years.

It wasn't the ideal start to my love life, but I have never wanted to be defined by any of my relationships. Some of my personal relationships were disastrous, some were important learning lessons, while others turned into lifelong friendships.

When I was living in Adelaide, I went out with an AFL player named Peter for many years. That was more a beautiful friendship than a sexual relationship. We used to go out to parties and the cinema, or we'd go water skiing, or I'd watch him play football – all very innocent. I had many friends in Adelaide, but they weren't romantic relationships; I didn't have a lot of time for romance. As I was training so hard, I was only allowed to go out once a week, and that was the way I lived. I was very focused on my work, and happy to be, because I wanted to succeed in swimming.

When I moved back to Sydney, I went out with a guy named Ken Robinson from Rozelle. We became engaged in 1960, before I went to Rome. When you put the ring on the finger, it's all very exciting, but I quickly realised I didn't love him enough to marry him. I spoke to my dad when I got back, and he said, 'If you feel like that, you've got to break it off.' Dad agreed he wasn't the right person for me – Ken worked at Cockatoo Island with him. So I broke it off. That was a very short engagement.

In Rome, I went out with Keith Whitehead, the Australian water polo player, a little, and we had a beautiful time together – he took me around Rome in a carriage. But I was engaged to Ken, so of course there was no sexual relationship, not to mention that, even if I had been tempted, I didn't want to fall pregnant. We didn't know about contraception in those days, because it wasn't talked about or freely available. Nowadays, you would be naïve to say there was no sexual activity going on in the Olympic Village – when you have a bunch of athletes with finely tuned bodies in close proximity, you'd expect sparks to fly. In my day, there was very little crashing of the girls' village (not that the chaperones would have noticed), but the weather was warm and there were plenty of open spaces to let nature take its course, for those who were so inclined.

As for me? Well, I was married to my sport. Water was the love of my life.

In the mid-1970s, I was contacted by a screenwriter, Joy Cavill, who had worked with Lee Robinson on the 1964 documentary we filmed in Tokyo. Joy wanted to make a feature film about my life, so I started going over to her house at Paddington. She would record my recollections and we'd talk. Then, surprisingly to me, and almost embarrassingly at first, our relationship became physical. Joy was 15 years older than me, and could be very motherly and nurturing, which I probably needed after losing my own mother a decade before. She also opened me up to the artistic and cultural sides of life, which I enjoyed exploring.

Looking back on that period, it wasn't really who I was, but the relationship was good for me at the time, and helped me get through a tough stretch in my life. Joy gave me good advice and I know I was a physical attraction for her. I didn't know how to handle it at the time, and she tried to teach me, but I was always uncomfortable. The relationship eventually petered out. We had very little in common and I didn't crave her company as I had with my husband Gary, or with Graeme Langlands.

I wanted to explain all this in my biography, but I had to discuss it with my daughter first, who was all grown up by then. She had an inkling of the story, but didn't know the whole truth, and I couldn't have lived with myself if I wasn't honest with my family.

I asked Dawn-Lorraine to get all the family together. 'I'm going to get five kilos of prawns and some beer and we're going to fill 'em up and talk about this,' I said.

She said I didn't have to do that, but I wanted to. I knew some of the revelations might hurt people, but we had to talk about it and move on, and I felt I had to write about it.

When everyone was gathered, I began with, 'Dawn-Lorraine and I have something to tell you.' My daughter took my hand and squeezed it. 'You know we're writing my biography,' I went on, 'and I said from the beginning that it would be a true account of my life. There won't be a lie in it, but there'll be parts of my life you probably won't have known anything about. The main thing I want to speak to you about tonight is that I had a relationship with a woman.'

'So what?' they said calmly. 'It makes no difference to us.'

Some people have said since that when I first spoke about the relationship, it was very brave of me, but I don't know why they think so. I wasn't into the 'gay scene' and I wasn't coming out of the closet, but it was an important part of my life and I am not ashamed of it. It was who I was at the time, and it was the right thing for me then.

I was disappointed with the film *Dawn!* when it was released in 1978. It tended to reinforce the myths and misconceptions about my life, and amalgamated too many characters, which wasn't fair to the people who'd played a big part in my success. The 'Dawn' character had feelings for the coach, and of course that never happened, although I do regard Harry as one of the most important people in my life. My mother's death, and my injuries and subsequent recovery, were not handled well either. In the scenes shot in Tokyo, they showed me climbing up the flagpole in the Emperor's Palace, which also didn't happen.

I had big arguments with Joy about the script. 'It will sell the film,' she told me, but if it did, I certainly didn't see any of the profits. I was supposed to receive a percentage of the film profits, but I guess there weren't any. Joy also wrote her character into the last third of the film, which did make me wonder if our relationship was more about fulfilling her artistic needs than out of any real caring for me.

Since the 1980s, I have had no significant relationship, just a series of close friendships I value enormously. That hasn't worried me at all – I view myself as a free agent. I can go anywhere I want, whenever I want, and I don't have to answer to anyone. My life is full and I have no regrets.

People have different relationships at different stages of their lives. Some might be fleeting, some might be mistakes, some might even be abusive. The main thing is to be smart enough to learn from them.

chapter 16

Serve your community

GROWING UP, AS WE DID, IN THE WORKING-CLASS SUBURB OF BALMAIN, MY PARENTS WERE ALWAYS LABOR SUPPORTERS, AS WAS EVERYONE WE KNEW. The Labor Party was formed in Queensland in the 1890s, but Balmain was the oldest branch and the district was ALP to the core. In the 1970s and 1980s, NSW Labor Premier Neville Wran lived in Balmain, and Labor held this safe electoral seat for most of the last century.

I wasn't that interested in politics until I took up swimming. Looking back, my first political action was probably in standing up against the Australian Swimming Union as a 12-year-old. Since then, I have railed against the unfair rules of officialdom all my life, but I left school at age 14-and-a-half, so I knew nothing about Australian history and laws or how State and Federal Governments operated.

In 1988, I was approached by some people in Balmain who were sick and tired of nothing being done about the problems in the area. These were very staunch Labor people who had become disillusioned with the party. I used to do a lot of work for the pensioners around there – that's how I was bought up, to look after the older generation and help out where I could – and I get on well with older people. Their main worries were that they'd had their free bus travel taken from them; there were few disabled facilities in the district; and the bus stops were placed too far apart. Labor did all of that, and in doing so, changed the very fabric of the community.

'There's an election coming up, Dawn,' they said. 'Why don't you stand?'

Years before, I'd gone to the Labor Party headquarters in Rozelle and said I wanted to join, but the head of the branch there told me I was too well known. 'Go away and come back when you're not that famous,' he said.

It was an amazingly stupid thing to say, and that was the end of it for me. 'I guess I will never join the Labor Party,' I told him, 'because I will always be well known.'

I started to think seriously about standing as an independent candidate. It made sense to me – I was an independent person generally, as well as a community-minded person. Rather than blindly following the 'party line', I could vote for whoever had the best policies to help my community. I started talking to local people and was encouraged to give it a shot. When I eventually announced I was running for Balmain, the Labor Party had been in power in the area for more than a decade.

I didn't even know how to register as candidate, but I had a lot of people putting their hand up to help me. I ended up with a very good team behind me – my friend Jim Gilchrist was my campaign manager; a successful local businesswoman (and staunch Labor supporter) gave me some good advice; and John Singleton quickly came on board, at a time when his advertising company had the account for the Labor Party. He did all the publicity for me, even making up all the posters: 'Our Dawn for Balmain'. I ran on the platform of being the voice for the people of the electorate.

In the election, Labor was ousted by Nick Greiner's Liberal Party and I was one of seven independents voted into office. I won the seat of Balmain because I was honest with them – the Australian public would not just vote for my name. I was well known in my community, but when I became the member, I went into other communities, such as Leichhardt, Lilyfield, Glebe, Annandale, Rozelle and Haberfield, speaking at schools and sporting events, fetes and community get-togethers, and telling people what I stood for. 'Is there anything you want me to speak about on your behalf?' I would ask, and there was always a long list of important issues. People wanted a voice and they believed in my ability to be that voice.

I enjoyed working in the NSW Parliament. They were very long hours and I worked hard. I was a true independent, not afraid to speak my mind or admit when I made a mistake. For example, I originally backed the Greiner government's decision to take planning powers away from Leichhardt Council, but later changed my mind and backed the locals, who opposed the redevelopment of the Balmain peninsula and foreshore. I was criticised for that, but at least I admitted to getting it wrong. Politicians are often too scared to change their minds on issues, while others are downright liars, who'll say anything to get votes.

The Labor Party, of course, was very bitter that I had won the seat from them. People would pass me in the corridors of Parliament, saying, 'You're only going to be here one term, Fraser.' I found out the members had their favourites with the press, so when I would call a press conference to announce some bill, the Labor journos would tell their colleagues not to bother going and I'd only have one reporter there. Dirty tricks indeed! I didn't complain in the press, because I was sure no one would believe me.

I was also one of the first women in parliament to wear pants. I was always well dressed, in a beautifully tailored pantsuit, but I'd still cop criticism. Once I asked the Speaker of the House, Kevin Rizolli, if I doing anything wrong. I had gone to see him earlier about my wardrobe, and he'd given permission for me to wear pants, but I explained that the other side were still having a go at me. 'We'll see about that,' he said. The next day, women on both sides of the floor were in trousers.

I think I am a very logical person. In coming to a decision, I would listen to both sides, then make my mind up. I spent a lot of time in the chamber, often just sitting there by myself, listening to the debate. There might only be one person from the opposition there (the Speaker is present all the time, of course) but I spent as much time as I could in the chamber, because I wanted to understand and learn about all the issues. I *had* to know about the issues, because I had to vote on them, and I only had my own opinion to go on. Sometimes I was frightened to leave the chamber in case I missed something important. If somebody asked me a question later, and I said, 'I don't know, I had to take a break when they covered that' ... well, that just wouldn't have been good enough!

Soon enough I was getting bills through and the major parties started taking notice. With the Beachwatch and Harbourwatch programs, I involved people who were interested in keeping our waterways clean. Locals would walk their dogs in the park adjoining the Dawn Fraser Baths, and when there was a heavy rain, all the dog mess would rush into the pool. This would close it for a week, because the bacteria level was too high. I was determined the council had to do something about it, and they did.

I made friends on both sides of the chamber, but many wished I would keep to sport-related issues, or issues confined to my local electorate. I had a terrible battle with a government minister once over the issue of Aboriginal rights at a coal mine. I knew this minister wanted the area redeveloped, but I wanted it to be saved, because I felt the history had to be preserved. Outside the chamber, when I suggested he make it a heritage site, he turned to me and hissed, 'I don't give a fuck about Aboriginal heritage.' Lovely.

I served in the NSW State Parliament for 3 years, 1 month and 15 days. During my period in office, I was criticised for going to the Seoul Olympics (I was given special leave because the Australian Bicentennial Authority had appointed me an ambassador) and for being too close to Premier Nick Greiner. I then had to deny a story circulated before my re-election that I was taking bribes from Kerry Packer, of all people, because he supposedly wanted to redevelop a chemical factory into a residential complex. I only knew 'KP' casually and the story was laughable, but after that stories were spread that I was in the pockets of property developers, who were financing my campaign.

In the 1991 election, the State Electoral Commission redistributed the boundaries of Balmain and Labor reclaimed the seat. I was disappointed, because I wanted to serve two terms and continue the work I'd started. I had learned a lot in that time and I had some of my projects up and running already. It had given me so much satisfaction to serve my community.

A young lass who was doing her HSC emailed me recently and asked me what makes a good leader. I told her it's someone who is honest – honest with themselves and honest with others. I was told a long time ago that if you're going to lie, you need a good memory, because you'll be easily caught out. And I don't have that kind of memory.

Politicians are shallow … they'll say or do anything to get elected, then change their minds and don't deliver. Make sure you vote for someone who, when they say they will take a bill into parliament, they actually do.

To my mind, there's little class or statesmanship in politics anymore. Julia Gillard backed down on so many electoral promises. And why did Kevin Rudd put a picture of his shaving cuts on Facebook? Bob Hawke was a larrikin, but he had class – you wouldn't see Hawkey putting himself on Facebook!

chapter 17
Acknowledge your achievements

In 2013, the Sportswomen's Ball at Parliament House, Canberra, sponsored by the Australian government, announced the top 100 Australian female athletes of all time. I was so proud to see my name at the top of the list, ahead of Betty Cuthbert and surfer Layne Beachley. The top 12 were rounded out by amazing female athletes: Margaret Court (tennis), Lauren Jackson (basketball), Heather McKay (squash), Rechelle Hawkes (hockey), Shirley Strickland (athletics), Anna Meares (cycling), Cathy Freeman (athletics), Karrie Webb (golf) and Liz Ellis (netball)

'We set examples for the younger generations to follow,' I said at the time. 'Times have changed drastically, which has been very good, and I would like to think that I was one of those people that changed those rules.'

Looking back on my career, I think I was something of a pioneer in the sport of swimming, particularly for women, at a time when there wasn't much money available to elite sportspeople.

After some sporting disasters in the late 1970s, Australia was looking to rebuild our international sporting reputation, and hoped to draw former Olympic champions like myself back into the fold. It was not so much the government who did this, but various sporting bodies around the country. The Australian Institute of Sport was set up in Canberra after our disappointing performance in the 1976 Montreal Olympics, and as we entered the 1980s we were virtually starting from scratch. We had to find new managers, coaches, administrators, physiotherapists and doctors, and develop a whole new system of reaching out to young athletes and training them in a systematic way. It would have been easy for me, and a number of other athletes who had been burnt by officialdom over the years, to say no thanks, but that was never my go. If I was asked to help, I would help.

In December 1985, the Sport Australia Hall of Fame was established to recognise Australian athletes of all sports and eras, and was later expanded to include people in supportive roles. On 10 December, 120 members were inducted into the Hall of Fame, including Sir Donald Bradman as the first inductee, and yours truly as the first female inductee.

To further acknowledge the achievements of our country's sporting champions, the Hall introduced a 'Legend' status, with one member being elevated to this level each year. I was granted legend status in the foundation year, along with 24 other athletes, including The Don, Sir Jack Brabham, Betty Cuthbert, Herb Elliott, Rod Laver, Evonne Cawley (Goolagong), Margaret Court, Reg Gasnier and Johnny Raper, plus fellow swimmers Shane Gould and Murray Rose.

In the Bicentennial Year of 1988, a Hall of Fame dinner was held simultaneously in Melbourne and Sydney, the two being linked up via television. At that function, the greatest male and female sporting performances of the last century were revealed, along with the greatest team performance. Bradman's 309 in one day (for NSW in 1930) and my third gold medal for the 100m in Tokyo got the nod, as did *Australia II*'s America's Cup win in 1983.

I like the ideals of the Hall of Fame – 'to preserve Australia's rich sporting heritage by honouring these great athletes, and use the values and experience of our Members to inspire our future stars'. I had visited many of these sporting institutions e around the world over the years and we wanted to make Australia's Hall a special place that anyone could visit. As a foundation member, I was automatically appointed to the Executive Board, and had a good working committee to start with. In 1995, when Sir Hubert Opperman retired, I was nominated as president of the Hall of Fame and spent the next five years working hard to make its ideals a reality.

There were a lot of politics involved, with different people trying to take charge, and in the end we weren't able to secure our own venue. We looked at various sites and had different plans over the years, but by the time the Sydney Olympics rolled around, we still didn't have a suitable venue in place. The Melbourne Cricket Ground had provided a room where we could display items of historical value, but we never got any revenue out of that. I thought that was unfair, as the MCG charged people to go in and have a look at the items on display. I never gave them any of my memorabilia for that reason – all of my items are in the International Swimming Hall of Fame at Fort Lauderdale, Florida. I get an invitation every year to go over there and meet the inductees, and reunite with old swimming friends. If I have the time, I love doing that.

There wasn't a lot of sponsorship available, so we had to be very careful with our funds. We invited Lionel Rose, a real character, to a function in Melbourne and he asked me if he could get a taxi home. As he'd made a special effort to get there, I thought it was the least we could do for him, so I gave him a taxi voucher. When we got it back, it was over $900 – Lionel had decided to go bush somewhere! The committee wasn't impressed and tried to wear me down about it, but I'd promised we'd pay his fare home, so we did.

I eventually fell out with Sport Australia's Hall of Fame because two members accused me of taking money and giving it to one of our committee members. These were legitimate expenses and the man in question needed to be compensated. I have never stolen money – except once when I was a very little girl and got the biggest belting of my life – and I haven't spoken to the two members since. I also resigned my place as the inaugural female inductee. Beyond this drama, my main criticism of the way the Hall of Fame was being run was that

I felt we couldn't go on having annual dinners and induction ceremonies when we still didn't have a home to call our own.

The new chairman, John Bertrand, is doing his best and is a courteous man for whom I have a lot of respect. He recently wanted to use my name for a certain promotion and wrote to me personally asking if he could. I told him it would be an honour and also explained why'd I kept my distance all these years. They recently invited me to their annual dinner, which I attended. I think they were pleased to see me there and I was pleased to be there, too. They've asked me to come again and I just might.

The Sport Australia Hall of Fame is still at the MCG, but who knows what will happen in the future? Sir Don Bradman has his own museum in Bowral, and John Singleton wanted to start one for me in Balmain, but couldn't find the right spot, which was a shame. I still have that idea in the back of my mind – a Dawn Fraser museum somewhere, with all my memorabilia and sports awards on show, so people can come and enjoy them.

In November 1999, as the 20th century drew to a close, I was nominated for the Athlete of the Century Awards, which were being represented by the World Sports Academy in Vienna. More than 10,000 journalists from around the world had nominated athletes in selected fields, and the nominations were decided by a panel headed by IOC President Juan Antonio Samaranch. Eleven other women had been nominated in the swimming category. All the athletes were invited to attend the presentation, and six other Australians were included – Betty

Cuthbert, Mick Doohan, Heather Mackay, Margaret Court, Sir Donald Braham and Rod Laver.

I accepted the offer of a trip to Vienna with Dawn-Lorraine and we made plans to visit our friend Andraz Vehovar in Slovenia along the way. Andraz won silver in the kayak event at the Atlanta Olympics and Dawn-Lorraine and I got to know him and his wife quite well. When we arrived in Slovenia, I learned that Leon Stukelj, the Slovenian gymnast with whom I had shared the stage at Atlanta, had died. I attended the funeral with Andraz the next day as a guest of the Slovenian government. It was very gracious of them to do that for me.

After a week with our friends, we rushed back to Vienna for the awards at the State Opera House. Dawn-Lorraine and I were dressed to the nines that night – the organiser had supervised our outfits, hair and makeup – and the excitement started to build once we saw all the press and the great athletes of the world assembled at the function.

While I was sitting there, waiting for them to announce the winners, I suddenly realised I was surrounded by millionaires. I am sure every single person in that room had struggled and sacrificed to become a champion, but many of the nominees for their respective sports had been paid millions of dollars in prize money – in tennis, basketball and boxing, for example. Sport was truly amateur in Australia, while the Americans were paid a lot of money for their success, even in my time. I heard that Mark Spitz got a million dollars for each of his seven gold medals at the Munich Olympics, which would have set him up for life. The AOC does the same today, giving out huge bonuses for golds. There wasn't anything like that for me – I worked three jobs to make ends meet, and to be able to train and attend the Olympics – and the swimmers I competed against at the Olympics were amateurs, just like me. I like to think I represented all of them in Vienna.

The winners were Alain Prost (motor sports), Steffi Graff (ball sports), Michael Jordan (ball sports), Nadia Comaneci (women's athletics), and Carl Lewis (men's athletics). Then the female water sports winner was announced, by swimmer Michael Gross.

'It's the one who came the longest way,' he said, 'Dawn Fraser.'

I went up on stage, where I received a huge crystal trophy, and somehow the words of thanks tumbled out of my mouth. If I hadn't realised I was a pioneer in world sport before, I think it came to me when I sat down with this beautiful award. Somehow I got it back home – via Mexico, where I had to stop over for a meeting with the World Olympic Medallist Association – and when I arrived back in Australia, my award was recognised with a civic reception at Town Hall held by Frank Sartor, the Lord Mayor of Sydney.

My award also led me to become a member of the Advisory Board of the World Jury for the World Sports Awards Foundation, which makes the final selection of nominees for the various sports categories and raises money for charity through the awards dinners. I was also invited to become a member of the World Sports Academy, which holds the annual Laureus Sports Awards annually.

It has been wonderfully gratifying to have this recognition in my later life. Two awards in particular that meant a great deal to me came a long way apart. Back in 1965, I was made a Member of the Order of the British Empire (MBE), but I was so broke I couldn't afford to travel to England to receive it from the Queen. Then, in 1988, I was appointed an Officer of the Order of Australia (AO). I gave these medals to my grandson Jackson, and he took great delight in showing them to a Japanese exchange student who stayed with us recently. The poor lad was wide-eyed. 'You won all that?' he asked.

Not bad for a Balmain girl!

chapter 18
Become a mentor

SINCE I STOPPED COMPETING, I HAVE REGULARLY BEEN INVOLVED IN CONVERSATION AROUND THE OLYMPICS. I usually have an opinion on decisions made about the Games, and when I do, I make sure my voice is heard! I especially wanted, after my retirement, to be a figure of support for young athletes as I believed my experience could help guide the way for them or help set policies that would be in their interests.

In 1980, when the Soviet Union invaded Afghanistan, US President Carter made the decision not to send an American team to compete in Moscow that year. Carter also encouraged other countries to boycott the Olympics and Malcolm Fraser's Australian government intimated it wouldn't fund a team.

I was against politics in sport, so I set up a fundraising group that raised $35,000 to help our athletes get to Moscow. The

AOF ultimately voted 6 to 5 to send an Australian team, but I was angry at the time that Prime Minister Fraser appeared to be hypocritical – he was apparently happy to sell wool from his family property at Nareen to the Soviet Union – and his government paid some athletes compensation not to go. I know the press had a bit of fun with the 'Fraser v Fraser' stoush, but it was quite a divisive issue at the time. I found myself receiving death threats and Dawn-Lorraine had to be escorted from boarding school.

I was invited to attend the games as the guest of the Moscow Organising Committee. The Russians were great hosts and I saw a lot of the country in the three weeks I was there. I had a driver and an interpreter and was provided access to the whole city, as well as to Kiev, Georgia, Leningrad and Stalingrad, which fed my appetite for historical sights. Although Australia did not officially boycott the games, only 120 competitors (92 men and 28 women, about half the usual squad) took part in the Games. But when we won our only two gold medals in the pool – Michelle Ford in the 800m freestyle and the men's 4 x 100m medley relay – no one cheered louder than me. All five bronze medals won at those games were collected in the pool too. The kids did great.

I had long entertained the thought of gaining a position on the Board of the Australian Olympic Federation (now the AOC). I had discussed as much with David MacKenzie, a close friend who had been Australia's Chef de Mission in Mexico in 1968, and was vice-president at the time of his death in the early 1980s – but the role never eventuated. I was so far on the outer with the AOF that I was not invited to the Los Angeles Olympics in 1984, but I went with John Singleton, who was commentating for Radio 2KY. We talked our way into the opening ceremony and broadcast our show from the lounge room of his friend, singer Rod McKuen. I stayed at the Ambassador Hotel and met up with Jan Andrew and her husband, the triple international Dick Thornett (rowing, rugby and rugby league). We had so much fun.

In 1988, I was appointed a Bicentennial Ambassador by the Australian government, and travelled to Seoul as an athlete liaison. I was invited to march in the opening ceremony by the AOC's John Coates and provided with an Olympic blazer, which I was proud to wear. It had been 24 years since I marched in the Tokyo Games and it felt wonderful to be back.

I really believed I had something to offer the young athletes, after surviving so many run-ins with officialdom over the years, and thought I could help them settle into life at the Olympic Games. I was asked to be involved with the swimmers, of course, but also women's water polo and the equestrian team; Vicki and Wayne Roycroft had asked for me, and with my love of horses, I was delighted to be with them. The women's basketball team were also having difficulty settling down in Seoul. Many had never been away from home before and were missing their partners, so they weren't playing well. I talked to them about focusing on the job at hand and many of them shared their innermost fears about competing on the world stage. I remember saying that if they went home without giving it their all, they would always regret it, because they might never get the opportunity again. They finished in fourth place and I know they gave it their best shot. I'm proud to say that all the groups I worked with in Seoul did their absolute utmost, though we only won three golds that year (Duncan Armstrong in the pool, Debbie Flint-off King on the track and the Hockeyroos).

It's not easy living in an Olympic village; in fact, it's probably the hardest living conditions for athletes. You have to learn to share your space and how to behave with your roommate, because your roommate is also your competitor. I know Lorraine Crapp and Ruth Everuss found it very hard to share with me in Rome, because I was a fierce competitor, but I became good friends with them both in the end. There was a good separation between the way we were in our living quarters and the way we were in the pool.

In Rome, a roadway had been built over the women's quarters. The men used to get out there with their binoculars and look into our rooms, and we had lot of fun giving them 'brown eyes' and generally being cheeky. We were all larrikins, but there was always a stopping point. If I was swimming that day and wanted to sleep, I would tell the girls, 'These are my rules. I want to sleep from 11am to 1pm. I want to get up and have my meal. I want to come back to bed at 3pm. I want to be on the bus at 5.30pm to go and do my warm up. That's my plan; please don't interrupt it. Now, what's your plan for the day?'

If they weren't swimming until the next day, they would go out, and when they came back, they'd go to the manager's room or lounge room so as not to wake me up. There were all kinds of routines like that to sort out.

In 1992 I went to the Barcelona Games in the official capacity of Athlete Liaison Officer, along with the great Herb Elliott, and worked mainly with the swimmers and the equestrian team. This was no sightseeing tour – it was a very hands-on role, caring for the horses and talking to the athletes in competition – and my days were stretched to the limit. My daughter came over too, and got a job 'kitting out' the Australian competitors, but I didn't see her much at all during competition. Imagine my surprise when I spotted her marching with the Australian team in the closing ceremony, wearing the uniform of an official who had decided not to take part. They do say the acorn doesn't fall far from the tree!

By 1996, I was certainly slowing down a bit. I had suffered a mild heart attack while working on my hobby farm in the Riverina and put on a little weight during my late fifties. But when I was asked by the AOC to be an Athlete Liaison Officer again for the Atlanta team, I couldn't say no, and was very excited about the Games being back in the United States. When I picked up my uniform, though, I realised there were no official badges on the blazer. I asked if there had been a mix-up and was informed that there were instructions not to put the Australian and Olympic crest on my jacket, because I wasn't really 'part of the team'. I was in tears when I handed the uniform back to them. I had represented Australia at three Olympics and in official roles in Seoul and Barcelona. They apologised profusely, but I was very hurt by it all.

What they didn't know, as it was all hush-hush, was that the Atlanta Organising Committee had confidentially invited me to the Games to take part in the opening ceremony. I was also invited to attend all the events and had the use of a driver, with all my accommodation taken care of. It was very humbling to be so well-considered by another country and this honour helped gloss over the thoughtlessness of the AOC, who had offered me another role as a VIP host meeting dignitaries. At the advice of my good friend John Singleton, I accepted it, and kept the generosity of the Atlanta committee to myself. The AOC might even have sent me the uniform with the Australian badge on it, but if they did, I never saw it, and I would not have worn it out of principle.

Once I was in Atlanta, I took on the role of VIP hostess with some gusto, meeting sponsors and parents of competing athletes, past Olympians and SOCOG members, and observing the Olympics, with a mind to our big day in the year 2000. The day before the opening ceremony, we had a rehearsal at the Olympic Stadium. There, I met the other athletes who were taking part in the ceremony – Bob Beamon, the Olympic long-jumper; Leon Stiukelj, the Slovenian gymnast and the oldest person to have won a gold medal; Nadia Comaneci, the great gymnast; and Carl Lewis, Mark Spitz and Greg Louganis, three of the greatest American athletes of the 20th century.

I was also asked by Coca-Cola, the official sponsor of the Games, if I would like to take a leg of the torch relay on the morning of the opening ceremony. My leg would take me past the Australian contingent at the Fox Theatre, which had been rechristened 'The Fosters Club'. The relay was delayed about an hour on the day and the weather was hot as hell. While we were waiting and trying to keep cool, a rather large lady tripped down the stairs and fell on my knee. I had to have it strapped, then faced a large hill when my relay leg was changed at the last minute. My knee was blowing up badly and I was going to pull out when I saw the hill in front of me, but then the adrenalin kicked in, and off I went.

My daughter and many of our Australian friends missed seeing me run the torch relay because of the last-minute changes, but I later grabbed an Australian flag and ran all the way from the Days Inn where I was staying down to the Town Hall behind the torch relay. I was just carried away with the moment, I guess! I spent the remainder of the day icing my knee before the opening ceremony that night.

Once competition started, I was very busy, and although I'd committed myself to meeting with coaches and athletes, I was feeling tired in the humidity. I was just about to head off to the pool and speak to swimmer Scott Miller when I felt pains in my chest, and I ended up spending the rest of the week in hospital, having suffered a mild heart attack. The doctors suggested I return to Australia, but Dawn-Lorraine and I had booked a seven-day cruise at the end of the Games and I didn't want to miss that. Unfortunately I remained unwell through most of that trip and couldn't wait to get home in the end.

What happened to me in Atlanta was a big wake-up call, health-wise. I was placed on a strict diet and had to reeducate myself about what to eat. Unfortunately, I found it hard to slow down and started feeling chest pains again when I was stripping wheat back on the farm. It was only angina, but the doctors impressed upon me the importance of not putting my body under undue stress or panicking if I did feel any pains.

As I turned 60, I lost some weight but when I found myself lacking energy and drive I was diagnosed with diabetes. Although I was scared of this misunderstood disease, I visited a specialist, who briefed me on what I needed to do. I could manage my diabetes with medication – there was no need for injections – which brightened me up. I was able to change my life and my lifestyle, and head off into the new millennium feeling positive.

Many young people don't realise that the people they meet today might well be able to help them in the future. Careers are over far too soon in sport and the money you earn is just as quickly gone. I think it's very rewarding to mentor others, and when I get the opportunity, I always enjoy it. I'm only sorry I wasn't a mentor to the swimming team in London … perhaps the results would have been different if the swimmers had more support on the ground.

chapter 19

Find your heroes and cherish your friends

BACK IN 1957, LORRAINE CRAPP, JOHN HENDRICKS AND I WERE INVITED TO HONOLULU, HAWAII, TO SWIM THE 400M AT THE KEO NAKAMA INVITATIONAL. There was a beautiful 110-yard saltwater sea pool there – it's fallen into the sea now, which is a shame. Swimming in a 100m pool was a different experience to the 25m and 50m ones we were used to.

It was Ricksy who pointed him out to me. 'There's your heartthrob over there,' he said one day.

'Who?' I asked.

'Tarzan,' he said.

Standing near the pool was the actor Johnny Weissmuller, all six-foot-six of him. He had been my hero since the days when my brother Donnie took me to see the *Tarzan* movies in the 1940s, but I also knew of his swimming background. Thirty years before, Johnny had won three gold medals at the 1934 Paris Olympics (100m, 400m and 4 x 100m relay) and two more in Amsterdam in 1928 (100m and 4 x 100m freestyle) before he got into movies.

'Isn't he wonderful?' I gushed. 'Oh, I love him so much.'

I was such a huge fan and I just had to meet him. Our coaches were telling us to get in the pool and train, but I was acting like a big kid.

Then something wonderful happened. Johnny walked over to me and asked, 'Are you Dawn Fraser?'

'Yes, Mr Weissmuller,' I mumbled.

'Just call me, Johnny,' he said.

I got over my shyness and we sat on the wall together, talking about swimming. When he swam the 400m in Paris, he had finished about four seconds outside the five-minute mark. Both Lorraine and I had broken five minutes for the 400m the year before, which amazed him.

'They used to think I was a freak,' he told me. 'You're just teenagers, and you're starting to make my times look slow.'

Johnny asked me if I knew how to swim a 100m pool and I shook my head.

'Well it's not a 50m pool, so don't go out too hard,' he said. 'Pick your spots to move up into the race.'

It was the first time I learned how to plan a race over a long distance. Later, we swam in a pool at San Francisco that was 440 yards long, which was even more difficult.

I broke two world records in Honolulu and won the Johnny Weissmuller Trophy as the swimmer of the meet. My hero presented the trophy to me and we spent a lot of time together over the five days we were there. We became so friendly that by the end of the week, I was calling him Tarzan, and I even had a swim with him. He was a true legend, one of the great icons of world sport.

I've been fortunate, in fact, to meet both my childhood heroes. In 1995, John Singleton organised a testimonial dinner for me with a percentage of the proceeds going to the Paralympics team who were travelling to Atlanta the following year. He and Kerry Packer arranged for Esther Williams and her husband Bill to attend as special guests. I had been a huge fan of Esther's since seeing her aquatic-themed movies, *Million Dollar Mermaid* and *Neptune's Daughter*, as a teenager in the 1950s, and had already met her a decade earlier, when I was inducted into the American Women's Sports Foundation Hall of Fame. She was a beautiful lady and I was flattered then that she knew of my career. 'You know, Dawn, I was the first swimmer to be inducted into the Hall of Fame,' she remarked.

'Ah, yes,' I replied, 'but I'm the first Australian.'

We hit it off straight away.

When she came to Australia for my testimonial, we spent ten days together, holidaying in the Hunter Valley. We swam every day and talked about film and life. She had a few airs and graces, because she was so famous all her life, but we got on great. Sadly, she passed away in 2013.

Interestingly, in the film *Million Dollar Mermaid* Esther played Australian swimmer Annette Kellerman, who overcame childhood illness to become a swimming champion and a star of stage and screen. Years ago, before her death in 1975, I met Annette and swam with her at her Surfers Paradise home.

I've been very fortunate during my career to meet so many important people and great athletes – from Queen Elizabeth II and Nelson Mandela to Muhammad Ali and Carl Lewis – and I've been able to share this good fortune with my daughter Dawn-Lorraine and grandson Jackson.

Every person I've met, from ordinary people to millionaires, has treated me like a long-lost friend. I liked Kerry Packer very much when I got to know him a little in the 1990s. He let me use his swimming pool in Park Street, because there were no heated swimming pools in Sydney. Another story I like about KP is when John Singleton organised a testimonial dinner for me in 1995. I was talked into putting the Olympic flag, given to me at the end of the Tokyo Olympics, up for auction, and I didn't want to do it, but because the function was also a fundraiser for the 1996 Paralympics team, I thought it was a good cause and might make some money for them.

I was sitting at the official table with my daughter Dawn-Lorraine, John Singleton and Kerry Packer, and my special guest Esther Williams, with her husband Bill. Dawn-Lorraine was very emotional about the idea of selling the flag – it was her legacy too, she said, and was bound to be valuable because it had 'historical importance'. As the bidding started in earnest, she got even more upset, and when the flag was sold for $52,000 to a 'mystery phone bidder', she was devastated. Then Kerry Packer took the flag and gave it to my daughter. 'You can stop fucking crying now,' he said, in his typically gruff manner.

John Singleton has been such a great friend to me over the years, and to so many other people, that I think of him as a knight in shining armour. I first met him at the races in the 1960s before he made his name in advertising and liked him straight away. He has a wonderful intelligence, a great sense of humour and he is very generous in his friendships. When we get together its larrikin on larrikin, and we've had some great times over the years, as well as sharing the bad times. After I left the pub in Balmain, for example, Singo acted as my unofficial manager, getting me various speaking engagements to help me back on my feet. I started off at small meetings for no payment, and graduated to large corporations, who were impressed enough to come on board as corporate sponsors. Singo has given me great financial advice over the years and I trust him completely. I could call him now, any time of day, and he would help me if I needed him, and vice versa.

John gets some bad press from people who don't know him. He's just a big softy, though, and a very lovable man. He has a strong kinship with Indigenous Australia and genuinely cares about people who are down and out. He supported Rev. Bill Crews and his Exodus Foundation at Ashfield for years – they're open every day of the year, with a hot meal ready for anyone who needs it, all out of his own pocket. Who else in Australia does that for strangers?

Like him or not, he's a good person and he's my friend.

I think I've been a good friend to a lot of people over the years and I've been able to maintain some of these friendships all my life. That's Dawn Fraser the person, not Dawn Fraser the

Olympic champion. I keep in contact with people – though it mightn't be for 12 months – and the friendships survive. The beauty of a real friendship is that you can take up the conversation exactly where you last left off.

Even successful people need mentors, close friendships and relationships. Fame is fleeting, and you don't know how long you're going to have it, but friendships are forever. And it's important to form friendships that are going to last.

When I had my car accident and my mother was killed in 1964, I never wanted to swim again. In my heart, I had been swimming to represent my family, but my Mum and Pop were gone. It was only because my teammates said, 'C'mon, Fras, we need you and you can do it,' that I even got back in the pool. That's true friendship and that's where my sporting nature fits into my personality. Swimming made me feel wanted, and without the help of fellow athletes, I don't think I would have been able to continue. If young sportspeople close themselves off from meeting others, they are closing themselves off from the key relationships that will help them in life.

When thinking about friends and heroes, and the dreams I have fulfilled in travelling the world and meeting so many interesting people, I can't help but think back to my childhood in Balmain, and remember the boy with the easy smile, who'll remain forever young in my memory. My original hero, my best friend, my brother, who would never get to see my success – Donnie.

chapter 20

Never cheat

FROM THE MOMENT IN SEPTEMBER 1993 WHEN SYDNEY WAS AWARDED THE 2000 OLYMPICS, THE GAMES PROMISED A LOT. When the time came, they also delivered a lot, although there were moments of disappointment. I have to be honest and say I was disappointed not to light the Olympic flame at the stadium on opening night. I suppose all the people who carried the torch into the Olympic Stadium that night thought, at one time or another, that they might be the chosen one, but in the end it was Cathy Freeman, who pulled it off magnificently, to her immense credit.

I did think it was a risk to put all that expectation on Cathy – it would have been easier for the AOC to place the burden of lighting the flame on a non-competitor, and I would have loved that person to be me. But I was proud I got to run around the stadium with the torch, and that I was the last person to hand it over to Cathy. The fact that she won gold, even under so much pressure, speaks volumes about her.

I was asked to be involved in our Olympic bid in 1991. Having finished my stint in state politics, I was keen for another challenge and I'd had such a long relationship with the Olympics – even to the point of doing my own fundraising to support the 1980 squad to Moscow – that I knew I had a lot to offer the organising committee. I worked hard on the bid, but when the time came to go to Monaco for the announcement, I wasn't invited. The unofficial feedback was that they didn't want any 'old athletes' hanging around, though who knows if that's true! Instead, I spent the night of the decision at a party at the overseas passenger terminal in Sydney. When the winning bid was announced – at 4.21 am – the whole place exploded into celebration.

The next seven years of planning were not without their hiccups. I was asked to be an Athlete Liaison Officer again, which I was happy to do for the swimmers, the water polo and the equestrian team, and was offered the role of attaché to the Sydney Olympic teams. When I was asked to take part in the Olympic Torch relay – something I had experienced in Atlanta four years before – I received conflicting letters assigning me to different venues in Sydney (first the Opera House, then George Street) but was resigned to this kind of error as part of the reality of planning a big event. When I discovered the same thing had happened to quite a few people, however, I was angry when the minister in charge, Michael Knight, said that no one had been promised a place in the relay. I told him of the two letters I had received, and he said I would be involved in 'other things'.

Then, on the day of my torch run – the day before the Olympics – I was called into the office of John Coates and told that Mr Samaranch, head of the IOC at the time, had asked for me to be the First Lady of the Games and to accompany him into the presidential box on opening night. I was happy to be First Lady, as it is an honour not many athletes have enjoyed. Mr Samaranch's wife was not well – in fact, very sadly, she passed away during the Games – and on the night, I warmed to the task of explaining the cultural references of the opening ceremony. I was impressed by his obvious strength at a very hard time.

At a given cue, I left Mr Samaranch's side and made my way to my position in the torch relay inside the stadium. Herb Elliott brought the Olympic flame in, then passed it to Raelene Boyle, myself, Betty Cuthbert, Shirley Strickland, Shane Gould, Debbie Flintoff-King and finally Cathy Freeman. Having to push Betty Cuthbert in her wheelchair was very difficult on that very hard track, as the cloth underneath the wheelchair was getting caught, so thank God I was strong enough to push through! I wasn't going to give up at that moment.

It was poignant seeing all the female athletes who were part of that procession, with all my old friends taking centre stage. I'm pretty sure it was not so much a feminist statement, though, as the fact that the girls had won so many more gold medals (sorry boys!). Or maybe it was a nod to us, that the officials had been a little hard on the girls over the years. It was a nice touch.

Of course, there was the glitch with the Olympic cauldron stalling. I don't know how I would have handled that, but Cathy showed great poise and presence of mind while the technicians fixed the problem. She got wet when the torch wouldn't light, and later I gave her my jacket because I didn't want her to get cold. As an athlete, she had to compete, so I had a lot of personal concern for her in that moment.

When I returned to the presidential box after the ceremony finished, the official party had already left. I returned home to my apartment at Homebush to meet up with friends before heading off to the Olympic Village and readied myself for the first day of competition.

The Sydney Games produced so many memorable moments, not least Cathy's wonderful win in the 400m final, but also teenager Ian Thorpe's success in the 400m, Grant Hackett's double in the pool, the men's success in the equestrian team event, Susie O'Neill in the 100m, the men's relay wins in the 4 x 100m and 4 x 200m relays, and the last-second win over America in the women's water polo.

I heard people remark what a shame it was that the 2000 generation of athletes didn't get a trip overseas for the Olympics, but I absolutely disagree. Just as we experienced in Melbourne in 1956, there is no better feeling than competing in front of your home crowd. It was a feeling that sustained me for 44 years and I never thought I would experience it again, but Sydney came close. It's also the best chance to medal, with the crowd carrying you through, and that's how it eventuated for our athletes with a record haul of 58 – 16 of them gold.

One of the terrible things to have come to light after the Olympics is that future generations will look back on those Games and know someone like Marion Jones cheated the system.

Drugs have been in sport throughout my career, but the effect it had on performances really became apparent in the 1960s. When we were training at Richmond leading up to the Melbourne Olympics, there was a lot of talk about swimmers taking drugs. It was easy to get paranoid about it and stories circulated that the Americans were seen 'sucking on oranges', then not throwing the oranges in the rubbish bin – the implication being that were injecting the oranges with something to give them a boost. If that was the case it didn't show in the results, because they won only two gold medals in Melbourne, but it gives you a sense of the paranoia.

At the Richmond Baths, I can remember our coach playing a joke on the Russian media, who were watching us train from the other side of the pool. He got Ricksy and me to get out of the pool, then hit us with a handful of Smarties and told us to swim as fast as we could. Afterwards, I hopped out of the pool like the Energiser rabbit, crying, 'Jeez, coach, that felt great!'

The emergence of drugs was no laughing matter though. In the 1970s, the eastern bloc countries – notably East Germany – undertook systematic doping of their athletes. It's fairly well documented that Raelene Boyle was pretty much robbed of a gold medal at the 1972 Munich Olympics, because the East

Germans doped their athletes. The Soviet swimmers in the 1980s and the Chinese swimmers in the 1990s – you only had to look at them on the blocks to know something was wrong.

Sprinters like Marion Jones and Ben Johnson, or the cyclist Lance Armstrong, will be branded as drug cheats for the rest of their lives. Shouldn't these be cautionary tale for anybody? But there are athletes out there still thinking, 'I'll beat them, I'll beat the system.' I don't think these can see the consequences ahead of them. The truth is, you can't beat the system – in ten years time, the technology will be even better than it is now – and why would you want to? What's the glory in an assisted win? You might make millions of dollars, but how can you sleep at night. If you've got a body and you train hard, you'll prove you can be the best in the world without any drugs, purely on your own merits.

The doping confessions of Lance Armstrong were a great disappointment to me. I saw him race and I admired him very much. 'What a magnificent athlete he is,' I thought. Then all of a sudden, he admitted what he'd done, and his whole reputation was gone. That should be a warning to anyone – if you build your success on a falsehood, you can lose everything, just like that.

chapter 21

Plan for the future

I VALUE MY PRIVACY. It's nice to be able to walk into a shopping centre and have a normal conversation with people. Of course, when people are polite and discreet, and want to say hello, that's always fine with me and has never been a problem.

There definitely seems to be a fascination among some younger people today with showing off and being seen at the right places – not to mention taking nude photos and passing them around on electronic media! But I would advise anyone to be careful about pursuing celebrity. For a start, it is fickle; if you're known for one thing, like appearing on a reality TV show, and you don't have something else to follow it up with, people won't be interested when you're not doing it anymore.

For athletes, it's very important to look to the future. If you think you have another ten years in the sport, you should really consider what you are going to do at the end of those ten years. I think many sportspeople see going into media as their best option, but for many the chance won't eventuate, or at least won't turn out to be a sustainable career. There are so many other avenues you can take these days, including going back to university to reskill.

Surround yourself with critical friends – people who are objective about you, but have your best interests at heart. Ask them to be honest with you and accept that they will be. I always had people around me who talked to me truthfully – my coach, my family, close friends – and their advice served me well. A lot of young sportspeople have managers and yes-people in their camps. I prefer someone to have a debate with me if they disagree, rather than just nod their heads at whatever I say; I don't want you to tell me I'm right, I want you to be honest and not bullshit me.

Often young people don't make plans, or have no Plan B, so when they get into trouble they don't know how to get out of it. They think it's the end of the world and can't see beyond the problem. I look back at my life and I can see that my mistakes and disappointments have inspired me to try harder and to be a better person. If you take a knock, get back up, put your back against the wall and analyse the situation. If it's not where you want to be, ask yourself where you went wrong and how you can rectify the issue. It's like if a lane isn't very good when you're swimming – you might as well try another lane.

It's also important not to be spoiled or wasteful with any money that comes to you. Money can be just as fleeting as fame, so utilise it sensibly, or put it away. Whatever you earn, make sure you've got your rainy day covered. In the real world, you don't get anything for free. People in the media and sports stars often get money so easily that they don't see the value of it anymore. It worries me that young sportspeople are paid so much. They have everything provided – accommodation, airfares, clothing, sponsors' goods – but they're not learning how to budget, save and invest.

I've even taught my young grandson to save his money. He does his chores and gets $5 a week, which goes into his savings account. Any money he gets, he puts in his moneybox, and once a month he takes it down to the bank. He's got nearly as much money in the bank as his Mum, these days, because he's such a good saver!

We were overseas recently and he saw some Lego that he couldn't get in Australia. The kit was over $100. 'I'll pay you back,' he said. I bought the Lego for him, and when we got home, the first thing he did was go to his moneybox and repay me. I know a lot of parents would be tempted to let it go, but there was a lesson in it – if you spend money now, it's not going to be there later on.

Young people are reaching a level of success and attention and yes, even celebrity, at an increasingly young age, but I think it's important to remember the simple fact that none of us are better than anyone else. I've tried to impress that on a lot of young kids I've met over the years. The rules still apply to celebrities and pride comes before fall. I was once told, 'all publicity is good publicity', but I learned over the years that bad publicity is *not* good publicity. The way the media is today, it's harder for young sports people to have privacy when they go out for a meal or a drink, but some people enjoy the limelight so much, they'll tell the media where they're going to be, and often, of course, it all goes wrong. They have a few too many, get annoyed with fans or end up in a fight. Is that good publicity? Be careful what you wish for, I reckon. If you want people to take photographs of you and put them on social media, that's fine, but you have little control of what happens to those photographs next.

Young kids need to realise that when they are grabbing publicity, they are also getting publicity for their sponsors. And your sponsor is not going to be very happy if they see you drunk at a nightclub on your Instagram or Facebook feed. They want the nice, clean image of you that they see in the swimming pool, receiving a medal or competing in a final. When an athlete gets bad publicity, the sponsor reassesses the situation and may well decide they don't want you. That could be a lot of money to lose – $100,000 can support you for two years when you're training.

If I was coming through the system now as an 18-year-old, I would be talking to prospective sponsors and asking about their expectations. Do you expect me, once a month, to come and talk to the company? What product signage do I have to wear in public and what functions do you want me to attend? I've lost sponsorships sometimes, or not had them renewed, but that happens in the commercial world. Things change quickly. I'm old enough to accept that now, but if that happened to me at the age of 19, I'd be asking myself some pretty tough questions: Where did I go wrong, and what didn't I do to get this sponsorship renewed?

Setting boundaries, which is something I've learned over the years, is also very important. When I was suddenly thrust into the spotlight, I was given the following advice by my father: 'If you go want to go out privately, do so. If you're recognised at a restaurant or in a bar and someone wants to take a photograph, you can say no, you don't want to be photographed in that environment. If you're having dinner or you're out with friends and you are approached for a photo or autograph, you may say no. If people think that's rude or standoffish, then you're sorry about that.'

At the same time, it's doesn't cost anything to be nice to people. When I took an NRMA Members tour to New Zealand for the World Cup in 2011, we went to a Wallabies training session, where I met Quade Cooper and James O'Connor, two young men who have attracted their share of bad press over the years. They could not have been nicer and I can't speak highly enough of how those two boys, along with their lovely coach Robbie Deans, treated us on that tour. Quade and James were a delight, asking my grandson Jackson if he was going to play rugby, and had their photo taken with him. The Wallabies showed they were sportsmen, not celebrities.

My good friend Marjorie Jackson is a prime example of someone who used her achievements as an Olympian as a springboard to serve the community. Marjorie won the 100m and 200m double on the athletics track at the 1952

Helsinki Olympics and was a great role model for the younger sportspeople like me coming through to the Melbourne Olympics. Marj married Olympic cyclist Peter Nelson and they had a cycling shop out at Unley when I was training there in the late 1950s. We became great friends and they used to take me to the drive-in movie theatre on Saturday nights.

Peter died of leukemia in 1977 and I worked very hard for the Leukemia Foundation with Marj over the years, having lost my brother Donnie to the same disease. Marjorie Jackson-Nelson became Governor of South Australia in 2001 and served her state with great distinction, aged in her seventies. She is a remarkable example to us all.

chapter 22

Be a team player

AN OLYMPIC GOLD MEDAL IS SEEN AS A GOLDEN TICKET TO A GOLDEN FUTURE. There is nothing wrong with striving to be the best, but it's important that individuals don't break away from the team. I believe some Australian swimmers forgot that at the London Games in 2012, and the net result was that we won only one gold medal. The United States, on the other hand, won 16 gold, 9 silver and 6 bronze medals. Many of the Americans, particularly the women, cited their 'close-knit team environment' as the telling factor in the team's success.

It was that obvious.

A lot of people see swimming as an individual sport. It's actually a team sport. Yes, there is individual success, but you celebrate as a team. I can remember each and every gold medal I won, because I shared it with my team. I remember coming back to my room in Rome and trying to be as quiet as possible, because there were swimmers competing the next day and I didn't want to disturb them. I found my bed short-sheeted and full of Smarties, then all the lights went on and the whole team was in my room shouting, 'Good on you, Fraser!' The girls who were swimming the next day had been moved to another area, and all the rest were waiting there for me.

It is important to act, behave and concentrate as a team, barrack as a team and support each other as a team, and it's apparent now that some swimmers at the London Olympics didn't show enough regard for their team members, which is an absolute disgrace. In the postmortems after the Games, it was found that competitors were overly focused on and affected by social media. If I was a young athlete starting out today, I probably wouldn't have much time for media. I'd close myself off, because I've learned over the years that the media are only writing stories to suit themselves and sell newspapers. I'd also throw away my mobile phone and hop off Facebook! And if I had been an athlete liaison officer, I would have said there were to be no phones at the pool, and banned phones altogether from anyone who argued with me.

It appears there was no cohesion or understanding of how to act as a team. If there are individual bonuses on offer for winning gold, and there are many, the focus can sometimes shift from doing well for your team to doing well purely for yourself. I think that happened in London. I felt for James Magnussen in losing the 100m freestyle by 0.01 of a second, but he later admitted that he went into the Games with the wrong mental approach, and it showed badly in his relay swim. I was appalled when he said in a news conference before the Games that he was 'the one everyone else had to beat'. The race had not been run yet, so that just put him under enormous pressure. He'd swum the race inside his head before he even hit the water.

It was also disappointing to hear allegations that the boys in the relay were knocking on doors at midnight. That's not fun, that's not larrikinism, that's just stupidity. After the Games, James Magnussen, Eamon Sullivan, Tommaso D'Orsogna, Cameron McEvoy and Matthew Targett all admitted to taking Stillnox during a team bonding session at a pre-London Olympics camp. 'Those people who take drugs in sport should be banned forever, not to ever be allowed to come back into the sport,' I told the press at the time. 'They should be punished severely because they are setting a bad example for the younger generation of our country.' I know my view on this shocked a few people. When my own past issues with Olympic officials were brought up, I said that being rebellious was entirely different to taking drugs in sport. 'Stillnox is an upper and I don't believe our swimmers should have mixed that with the drink that they did,' I said. 'I think they set a bad example. They wouldn't inspire me if I was a youngster coming up in the sport of swimming.'

I meant it, too.

I don't think specialised coaches have helped us, because we are not cohesive as a team. When our two long-distance swimmers showed up in Manchester to train with the squad, they were told by the head coach to go back to London, because there was no room for them in the pool. These were swimmers belonging to the Australian Olympic team being turned away. It doesn't matter if you're a 100m sprinter, a two-mile swimmer, an open-water swimmer – you need someone there to look at your stroke and coach you. It broke my heart to hear that. What does it tell those swimmers about their importance in the team?

How many friendships were made out of the London Olympics? All those athletes are having this wonderful experience at the same time; it's a communal experience. That's why, even in the competitive environment of an Olympic Games, you can still make life-long friendships. I can go anywhere in the world today and meet up with my Olympic friends.

In regards to Ian Thorpe's failed comeback bid before the Games – in my heart, I hoped 'Thorpie' would make it back. I think everybody did. But I couldn't see him doing it, because there were so many new kids swimming three seconds faster than he did at the same age in the 1990s. And he was a freak in his time! If you have twelve months out of a sport at that age, it's like having four years off, and it's very hard to make a comeback. If you are a sportsperson, the world passes you by very quickly, and there's always a new generation of kids coming along behind you. He also didn't stick with his old coaches, but moved on to new people, and I don't think they were tough enough with him, as he struggled with his times and he didn't qualify.

The worst part was that every little thing that went wrong was broadcast by the media. I could relate to the bad press he copped in his comeback; I often went home at night thinking, *What is the press going to write about me tomorrow?* Your name and reputation is very important to you as an athlete, and you have to protect it.

It appears Swimming Australia has cleaned out a lot of the management responsible for London and they'll start again. The signs at the 2013 World Championships were promising, but we have a long way to go to get back where we were in Sydney 2000 – or Melbourne in 1956 for that matter.

***

I wasn't offered a position working for the Australian team in London 2012. Whether I was too outspoken for Swimming Australia, or they just didn't want a 75-year-old getting in the way, I don't know. I was pretty much resigned to watching the whole thing on television. At the last minute, however, the Australian Olympic Committee's John Oates provided me with tickets to the swimming events, and my good friend Lindsay Fox and his wife said I should go, so they flew me and my grandson to London.

We watched the swimming and sat right at the finish line on the first level. I was in a motorised chair because it was a long way to the pool and my knee was playing up, and we were sitting near some American supporters. A toddler, about 18 months or two years old, came up to us and sat on my lap.

He took great delight in tooting the horn on my motorised chair during the races.

Well, the Americans turned out to be the family of Ryan Lochte, the gold-winning member of the US relay team, and the baby boy was his nephew. Ryan's mum and dad came up and thanked me for being so patient with their grandson, and asked if they could take a photo of the baby on my lap, which was lovely.

When Ryan joined the group after one of his swims, he said, 'Mum, do you know who that is? It's Dawn Fraser!'

'Oh my god,' they exclaimed, hurrying to remove the baby from my lap, but it was fine! It happens to me all the time.

chapter 23

Learn to grow old gracefully

My age never worried me – until I got older.

I always want to have a big, themed birthday party every ten years, just for the big 'zero' birthdays. I'm 76 this year and my grandson asked me, 'What's your next theme going to be, Grandma?'

'I don't know yet, mate,' I told him.

'Well, you haven't got long to think about it,' he said, 'so you'd better start planning.'

My eightieth birthday is still another four years away. If I start planning it now, it will go too quickly, and it'll feel like I'm 80 even sooner. I don't want to be 80 yet! It was all right when I was in my fifties, and I was planning for my sixtieth, and then my seventieth, but I don't want to be planning for my eightieth just yet. I just want to enjoy every day, and time does seem to go faster as you get older. I wouldn't mind if the years would slow down a little and take their time.

I've promised Jackson that I will dance at his 21st birthday. I want to keep my mind focused on that promise. Recently he said, 'I'm ten next month, Grandma, I've only got eleven years to go.' So I've got at least the next eleven years to keep myself fit and healthy. It doesn't matter if I'm confined to my bed in 2024 – I will somehow get up and dance at his birthday party, because that's a goal I've set myself.

The average age of people living today is between 82 for men and 85 for women. When I read the newspaper, I look through the funeral notices and note people's ages. I look at a person who was 82, and I say, 'That's not bad, that's a good life.' But I don't want that to be me.

I love walking. It keeps me vibrant. I don't walk as far as I used to, but I'm starting to get back into it. I have a friend coming back from overseas, who's just had five stents put in his heart, and I said to him, 'Right! We're going to walk every morning. We don't have to walk miles, but we'll walk up to the park and up the street and come back, and that's a good half-hour walk. We'll build it up and then we'll get to an hour's walk. It will be good for us – it's something that you've got to do for your heart to keep it going.' I can't stand to be a couch potato. If I sit on the couch and turn on the television after lunch, I'll be tempted to have a five-minute nap, so I'll get up straight away. A five-minute nap can turn into an hour's sleep pretty quickly, and I don't like sleeping the day away.

I got stopped in the shops the other afternoon. A little boy looked up at me with big eyes, saying, 'I want to be a swimmer.' I remembered I gave him a certificate last year, at the end of the season. I always do what I can to encourage these kids, asking them if they're going to join a club, and how many days a week they're going to go swimming. I'd like to think if I died tomorrow, those kids would say, 'Dawn Fraser helped motivate me,' and my name might live on with them.

I enjoy spending much of my time in Noosa, with my daughter and grandson. It's much easier for me, as my house in Balmain has thirteen steps to climb up into the lounge room, with another twenty-three to get up into my bedroom, and it's too hard on my knees. I find sometimes that if I've left something upstairs, I can't go back up, because it takes too much time. Living in Noosa, though, it's very flat, I can walk most places, and my daughter's house is all one level. My dog is very, very happy now that he's got a big backyard to run around in too. Jackson and I like to go out in a little dinghy and go down the river, taking the dog with us. We'll go fishing and have a swim, maybe lunch on the beach or something. Or we might go on a jet ski. I don't think there are too many 75-year-olds on jet skis down in Sydney, but I try and take advantage of the lifestyle up in Queensland. We're planning to go down to Stradbroke Island later in the year, where we'll spend four or five hours on the jet skis, so that will be great fun.

I'm the patron of Australian Ladies Professional Golf association and I play Masters Golf – it's nice to be able to feel like I'm still competing and to say that I have a sport. Back in 1962, when I won the Babe Didrikson Zaharias Trophy for

World Amateur Sportsman of the Year, I wanted to find out more about the award's namesake. As I discovered, Mildred Ella 'Babe' Didrikson Zaharias was an extraordinary woman who represented the United States in athletics, basketball and golf. After wining gold medals at the 1932 Los Angeles Olympics in the javelin and 80m hurdles, she became a champion golfer and an 'All American' basketballer. She died tragically of cancer at age 45. I also read that when Babe Zaharias took up golf, she practised her swing a thousand times, until her hands bled. I decided to take up the sport and followed her example, hitting a thousand a day until I could send a ball straight down the fairway. I've played golf for many years now and am always trying to improve my yardage – how far I can hit with a nine-iron, all the way down to a wedge. It also introduces me to a lot of interesting people and it's great exercise.

I've done a lot of travelling over the years, both inside Australia and internationally. I've been to Edinburgh and stayed with my Scottish relatives from Dad's side of the family. I didn't know much about my family until I started getting older, and I didn't grow up with grandparents, so it was nice to meet my Scottish cousins. Travelling overseas and meeting people who were related to me people motivated me to find out more about my family, and a relative in Scotland has traced Dad's side back to the 1500s, a pretty good effort considering Fraser is a fairly common name. I'd love to go to Peru and find out where Mum's side of the family comes from.

Jackson has visited his second cousins in Scotland and had so much fun there. We didn't see him for days, he was so busy.

A few years ago I had a sponsorship with a Winnebago company, and I promoted driving around Australia with a safari of 'grey nomads', from Queensland to Victoria. Unfortunately, I upgraded to an 8.7-tonne Winnebago and didn't realise that I had to upgrade my licence accordingly. The Gosford police pointed out the error of my ways, although the court declined to charge me, but at age 75 I now have the correct licence and have to do at least one trip in a heavy vehicle each year to maintain it. My daughter now has a heavy rigid license and can drive a bus with up to sixty people in it.

Having read this little book, you will appreciate that I have a very close relationship with my only daughter, Dawn-Lorraine, and her only son, Jackson. My daughter is smart, emotional, intelligent and headstrong, the person I argue with the most, and the person who knows me the best. We've been through a lot together over the years and there's many more adventures to come. I would have liked her to marry and settle down, something I didn't achieve during my life, and there was no shortage of proposals for either of us, but it was not to be. When she decided to have Jackson through IVF because the biological clock was ticking, I knew she would face criticism – by people who didn't even know her and even from some close family members – but she always had my unconditional love and support.

I don't know what Jackson's going to do with his life yet; he's only 10, so he hasn't made up his mind! He's very good with Lego, so maybe he'll be an engineer. He'll sit there with a whole tray of Lego and make a spaceship, with guns and rockets coming out the back, without plans or anything. He's also great on the computer and iPad; kids today really are amazing, with the technology they have at their fingertips. I love watching kid's movies with him – movies like *Toy Story*, *Monsters Inc* and *Happy Feet* are made with adults in mind as well these days. I enjoy them more than the mindless violence of adult movies, and it's nice to have that interaction with Jackson. I draw the line at 3D, though. It makes my head spin.

I've worked with many different boards and associations during my career. I am a director of Wests Tigers NRL Club, the Balmain Leagues Club, the Laureus World Sport Academy and the Save the Bilby Foundation. In addition, I am Patron of the Cerebral Palsy Foundation and the Noosa Triathlon and the Volunteer Lifeguard. I was a director of NRMA Limited from 1991 to 1995, after becoming involved in the Motorists Action Group that originally opposed demutualisation, and when the NRMA became a public company in 2000, I served as a director from 2005 to 2013. It was a big learning curve for me, passing the company director's examination and learning all the rules and regulations of being in charge of a major company. You want to do well by your members and make the right decisions.

***

I was not overly religious growing up, but I find I am as I get older. I went to Sunday School as a child, just across the road on King Street and Ramsay Street; it gave us kids something to do and kept us off the streets. All the children in the neighbourhood would get along there, especially if there was a birthday party to be celebrated, and somehow those early lessons seem to have sunk in.

Why are we here? What is God's plan for us? What happens when we die? These are great mysteries. Life is about reconciling with the fact that we won't ever really know the answers, and making every day count.

A lot of people turn away from religion, as they feel that the 'rules' are too rigid to follow. I would agree with that to some extent. I don't have to go to church every Sunday to know what is wrong or right. I have a soul inside of me, as I was taught by Mum and Dad, and I say my prayers at night. I go to chapel every Friday with my grandson and I love to hear the kids sing. I don't want my grandson to be forced into religion, I just want him to enjoy it. I'm happy as long as he believes in something in his own heart.

That's how I introduced my daughter to religion too. She went to Catholic school, so she knows more about that than her own Presbyterian faith; Jackson knows more about the Lutheran Church, because that's where he goes to school. But it all comes down to the same thing really. When we have dinner together, we hold hands and say grace. It's all very natural, and a part of growing up and growing older I think, so I'm all for it. I had an audience with Pope John XXIII when I was in Rome in 1960, and now he's going to be a saint. So I guess there's hope for all of us.

chapter 24
Stay true

I WAS RECENTLY IN SINGAPORE ON HOLIDAY WITH MY GRANDSON. The concierge at the hotel asked me if I had been there before, as I looked very familiar to him. I said, 'No, it's my first time here.'

'You have a very familiar face,' he insisted. 'I'm sure I've seen you somewhere before.'

I just smiled and said nothing.

We couldn't go out into the haze, because Jackson and I are both asthmatic, so we spent a lot of time inside the hotel. We came down to the mall in the hotel to do some shopping one morning when the concierge came up to me excitedly. He was holding a picture of me in his hand – he'd Googled me – asking, 'Is this you? Dawn Fraser?'

'Yes,' I said, 'that's me.'

'Oh my god!' he said. He went and told all the hotel staff that they had a famous Australian swimmer staying at their hotel, who had won many Olympic gold medals! It was a little bit embarrassing.

Later, Jackson and I were at the swimming pool when a Canadian gentleman and his wife came over and politely introduced themselves. He asked straight away if I was a swimmer. 'I used to be,' I said. 'How did you know?'

'I told my wife you must have been a very good swimmer once,' he replied. 'I used to teach children to swim, and your style is very unusual. You pull straight in the water and so does your grandson. Not many people do that. How good a swimmer were you?'

'I represented Australia at a couple of Olympic Games,' I told him.

'What's your name?' he asked curiously.

'Dawn,' I said.

'Are you Dawn Fraser?'

I nodded. He turned to his wife and exclaimed, 'I told you she was a good swimmer!'

We became good friends while we were there and had many chats while I was in Singapore. If I ever came over to Canada, he told me, I must stay with them.

I am often recognised on a personal level before people know my name, and that's just how I like it.

I'm not overly concerned about legacies. The name Dawn Fraser will always be there in the record books, which is really a wonderful thing to know. I look back on those achievements and realise that I was the first swimmer, male or female, to win gold medals at three Olympics in the same event. I was a young woman from the wrong side of the tracks who succeeded in a 'silvertail' sport, dominated by old men and officialdom. I was also named the female swimmer of the 20th century and that will live on long after I'm gone.

I'd like to be remembered as a pioneer in my sport, especially in terms of getting rid of the restrictions of amateur status, although I do sometimes wonder if it was a good thing in the end. It is great that young athletes today don't have to work three jobs like I did when I was competing for Australia, but once the doors were open, you couldn't stop the money coming in and it changed everything almost overnight. I hope the younger generation will learn that the money and celebrity and fame will take care of itself … but that hard work has to come first.

So what have I learned along the way? To be patient. To be compassionate. To be honest and forthright. If you say you're going to do something, do it.

Of what am I most proud? Mainly being a good person, a good parent, and a good grandmother. My daughter and my grandson will agree that there have been some trying times, but we've learned from these times together. The main lesson I learned was not to do anything wrong by them. I'm proud that I was one of eight kids in a working class family in Balmain, and achieved so much in my sport. I achieved everything in life through hard work – and it was my mother and father who instilled that in me. I'm proud of where the name Dawn Fraser sits in the Australian story and I'm proud that the name Fraser is known all around the world.

At this stage of my life, the most important thing for me is to set a good example for people of my vintage, but also for the younger generations. I have no thoughts of retirement and I have just signed a sponsorship contract for another five years. My health is very important to me, not just physical health, but also my mental health. You read so much about the onset of dementia, and how suddenly it hits people, so I think it's extremely important to remain alert and curious, and want to keep my wits about me. I read books, I attempt crosswords – I'm hopeless at them – and do Sudoku puzzles on my iPad. I'm also fascinated with squares. Whether that comes from my years of swimming and counting all the tiles on the bottom of a swimming lane, I don't know, but I'll often count the rows of tiles on the floor or walls of a room I'm in if I'm bored.

I've learned from disappointments during my life. When I was stood down from the Olympic team for twelve months after Rome, I served my time on the sidelines, then came back and trained hard and broke more world records. When I was banned for ten years after Tokyo in 1964, and the papers made it about something else, it took me years to accept that, but now I use those stories in my public speaking engagements at schools and corporate functions as lessons for others.

I also learned that when there are disappointments in life, it's not the end. My marriage ended very abruptly, but the cross-generational relationships I enjoy with my daughter and grandson are very strong, and it's important to me to prove that families can take many forms. The important thing is to make sure your relationships are stable, because if someone comes along and tries to knock it down, it has to be strong enough to survive.

There's no quick fix when things go wrong in life, but sometimes you have to get off your backside and do it. I did, so anyone can. If I want to buy something, I save up for it. I'm a person who has saved for anything I've ever wanted. I only buy what I can afford.

I write the word ENJOY on a pad every day and try and make an acrostic out of it. Each day it produces different words. I do this with school students and I get them to write down their words too.

E – Exciting and emotional
N – Naive, naughty and nifty
J – Jazz, job, justify
O – Olympic Games and opportunities
Y – You, yourself!

I've done that for years. When I was living in Adelaide as a young woman, I kept the word 'Enjoy' pasted behind my bedroom door, to motivate me to enjoy every day. More than 50 years later, that one word still has the ability to empower people.

Empower ... there's another word, right there.

When I look at pictures of me as my younger self, and I see a young girl, invariably hopping out of the pool, her thick hair dripping wet and a towel flung over the shoulder, I ask her: 'How did you survive all that? How did you do it?'

I survived because I stayed true to myself. And I loved every minute of it.

Records,
statistics and
honours

WORLD RECORDS

100 metres

Time	Date	Place
58.9	29.2.1964	Sydney, AUS
59.5	24.11.1962	Perth, AUS
59.9	27.10.1962	Melbourne, AUS
1:00.0	23.10.1962	Melbourne, AUS
1:00.2	23.2.1960	Sydney, AUS
1:01.2	10.8.1958	Schiedam, NED
1:01.4	21.7.1958	Cardiff, UK
1:01.5	18.2.1958	Melbourne, AUS
1:02.0	1.12.1956	Melbourne, AUS
1:03.3	25.8.1956	Townsville, AUS

200 metres

Time	Date	Place
2:11.6	27.2.1960	Sydney, AUS
2:14.7	22.2.1958	Melbourne, AUS
2:17.7	10.2.1958	Adelaide, AUS
2:20.7	25.2.1956	Sydney, AUS

AUSTRALIAN CHAMPIONSHIPS

Freestyle
110 yards freestyle: 1956, 1958, 1959, 1960, 1961, 1962, 1964
220 yards freestyle: 1955, 1956, 1958, 1959, 1960, 1961, 1962, 1964
440 yards freestyle: 1958, 1960, 1961, 1962, 1964
4 x 110 freestyle relay: 1957, 1958, 1959, 1964

Butterfly
110 yards butterfly: 1960, 1962

Medley
220 yards medley: 1959
4 x 110 yards medley relay: 1955, 1964

OLYMPIC GAMES

1956 Melbourne
Gold medal (2)
100m freestyle
4 x 100m freestyle relay

Silver medal
400m freestyle

1960 Rome
Gold medal
100m freestyle

Silver medal
4 x 100m freestyle relay
4 x 100m medley relay

1964 Tokyo
Gold medal
100m freestyle

Silver medal
4 x 100m freestyle relay

COMMONWEALTH GAMES

1958 Cardiff
Gold medal (2)
110 yards freestyle
4 x 110 yards freestyle relay

1962, Perth
Gold medal (4)
110 yards freestyle
440 yards freestyle
4 x 110 yards freestyle relay
4 x 110 yards medley relay

Awards and Honours
1964 – Australian of the Year
1965 – Inducted into International Swimming Hall of Fame
1967 – Named a Member of the British Empire (MBE)
1975 – ABC Australia's Best Sportsperson of the Past 25 Years (1951–75)
1981 – Awarded IOC Silver Order
1984 – Balmain Baths rededicated as Dawn Fraser Pool
1985 – Inducted American Women's Sports Foundation Hall of Fame
1985 – Inducted Australian Sporting Hall of Fame
1988 – Voted Australia's Greatest Female Athlete
1990 – Named a National Living Treasure
1998 – Named an Officer of the Order of Australia (AO)
1999 – Named World Female Swimmer of the Century
2000 – Awarded the Australian Sports Medal
2000 – Declared First Lady of the Sydney Olympics
2001 – 'Dawn Fraser Sports Award' inaugurated
2013 – Named Top Female Australian Athlete of All Time